Lovebirds

JULIE MANCINI

ANIMAL PLANET ♥ PET CARE LIBRARY

Lovebirds

Project Team
Editors: Ryan Greene, Craig Sernotti
Copy Editor: Stephanie Fornino
Interior Design: Leah Lococo Ltd. and Stephanie Krautheim
Design Layout: Stephanie Krautheim

T.F.H. Publications
President/CEO: Glen S. Axelrod
Executive Vice President: Mark E. Johnson
Publisher: Christopher T. Reggio
Production Manager: Kathy Bontz

T.F.H. Publications, Inc.
One TFH Plaza
Third and Union Avenues
Neptune City, NJ 07753

Discovery Communications, Inc. Book Development Team:
Marjorie Kaplan, President, Animal Planet Media
Carol LeBlanc, Vice President, Licensing
Elizabeth Bakacs, Vice President, Creative Services
Brigid Ferraro, Director, Licensing
Peggy Ang, Vice President, Animal Planet Marketing
Caitlin Erb, Licensing Specialist

Printed and bound in China.
06 07 08 09 10 1 3 5 7 9 8 6 4 2

Library of Congress Cataloging-in-Publication Data
Mancini, Julie R. (Julie Rach)

Lovebirds / Julie Mancini.
    p. cm. – (Animal planet pet care library)
Includes index.
ISBN 978-0-7938-3780-9 (alk. paper)
1. Lovebirds. I. Title.
SF473.L6M36 2007
636.6'864–dc22

2007009528

tfh

The Leader in Responsible Animal Care for Over 50 Years!™

www.tfh.com

Table of Contents

Chapter 1

Why I Adore My
Lovebird

Welcome to the exciting and fun-filled world of lovebird ownership! Lovebirds are active little parrots who enjoy entertaining their owners by playing in their cages or learning to do simple tricks. Hand-fed lovebirds are accustomed to people from the day they hatch from their eggs, and they like to cuddle with their owners. Lovebirds benefit greatly from daily interactions with their owners. Not noted for their talking ability, you can channel your lovebird's boundless energy into teaching him to do tricks.

The History of Lovebirds as Pets

People have been keeping birds as pets since the time of the ancient Greeks and Romans, and pet parrots were described by Persian and Indian writers more than 3,000 years ago. Explorers often brought home different bird species captured on their voyages in an attempt to please their wealthy royal sponsors and to make future expeditions possible.

The red-faced lovebird (*Agapornis pullaria*) was the first lovebird described by European explorers. It was described in the early 1600s, and it was the first lovebird species imported into Europe in the 19th century. Other species of lovebirds arrived in Europe in the 18th century by way of ships returning from Africa and Madagascar. The peach-faced lovebird (*Agapornis roseicollis*), for example, is noted in the 1793 edition of the British Museum catalog, although the species was grouped with the red-faced lovebird and not treated as a separate species at the time. By 1817, however, the peach-faced was being recognized and treated as a separate species from the red-faced.

By the mid-1800s, peach-faced lovebirds were being exported from Africa to Europe regularly. Other species followed, including the Madagascar (*Agapornis cana*) in the late 1800s, the masked (*Agapornis personata*) and the black-cheeked (*Agapornis nigrigenis*) in the early 1900s, the black-winged (*Agapornis taranta*) in 1906, and the Fischer's

(*Agapornis fischeri*) and the Nyasa (*Agapornis lilianae*) in 1926. Few reports exist of black-collared lovebirds (*Agapornis swinderniana*) being exported because this species did not survive quarantine well. The diet of black-collared lovebirds relies heavily on figs, and many birds died in quarantine because they were not able to eat this preferred food.

Europeans soon began keeping these charming little parrots as pets. They became popular aviary residents at many European zoos too because of their ease of care and readiness to breed.

Large numbers of lovebirds were exported from Africa to Europe and America in the early 1900s. Most of the nine lovebird species were represented

The Expert Knows

How Lovebirds Got Their Name

Scientifically, all lovebirds are considered to be part of the genus *Agapornis*. This word comes from the Greek words *agape* (love) and *ornis* (birds). It is believed that the birds were named "lovebirds" because of their natural habit of sitting close to one another and engaging in mutual preening.

in aviculture at that time, although six of the species are less commonly found in breeding collections or the pet trade today.

In the United States, lovebird breeding began in earnest in the early 1900s. A bird fancier in Cleveland, Ohio, named K.V. Painter was one of the early importers and breeders of both Fischer's and masked lovebirds. He began to bring both species into the country between 1925 and 1926. Painter's birds and other imported lovebirds settled into their new homes and began to produce offspring.

Lovebirds were one of the earliest parrot species to become established in American parrot breeding facilities, but other species were not as fortunate. By the 1980s, it was becoming apparent that captive breeding was the future for many pet bird species, and some forward-thinking breeders began to breed some of the rarer parrot species in captivity. In 1992, President George H.W. Bush signed a bill called the Wild Bird Conservation Act of 1992 that restricted the import of wild-caught parrots into the United States, so most pet birds sold today are captive-bred, domestically raised animals. (A few wild-caught parrots may still be sold by private owners through classified ads, but bird stores and breeders sell only captive-bred birds today.)

their heads and a slightly hooked beak that is somewhat large in comparison to the rest of their bodies. Beak color differs, depending on the species, and can range from a yellow–orange on the peach-faced to the bright red on the Fischer's and masked lovebirds to a delicate pink in some mutations. Some baby lovebirds have blackish beaks when they hatch, and their beaks lighten as they mature.

Why Use Scientific Names?

Due to the widespread popularity of pet birds around the world, many parrot species are known by several names, depending on the country in which they are kept. To simplify matters, serious birdkeepers often use scientific names when referring to different species of pet birds to ensure that they're talking about the correct bird.

What Americans call a peach-faced lovebird may be referred to as a rosy-faced or rose-headed lovebird in other parts of the world, but calling the bird *Agapornis roseicollis* eliminates confusion and helps you discuss that particular species more intelligently with other birdkeepers.

Body

A lovebird's height on the perch ranges from 5 ½ to 6 inches (14 to 15 cm), and he weighs between 50 and 70 grams (a range that is approximately 1 ¾ to 2 ½ ounces), depending on the species. Please note that avian veterinarians weigh pet birds in grams, rather than ounces, because grams are a more precise weight measurement, and even a slight weight loss can indicate a serious health problem in a pet bird.

Physical Characteristics of the Lovebird

Lovebirds are small, stocky parrots. They have large, dark eyes set on the sides of

A healthy lovebird will sit upright on his perch and hold his wings snugly against his body. His feathers will be smooth and shiny, and no bald spots will be visible between the feathers. His short, feathered tail will follow the slope of his back and wing feathers, and his tail feathers will be clean and unfrayed.

Despite his small size and stocky build, a lovebird is considered to be a swift flyer. For this reason, it's important to keep your pet's wing feathers trimmed to ensure his safety and to prevent him from accidentally flying away. We'll discuss wing trimming and other grooming topics further in Chapter 4.

Lovebirds are small, stocky parrots with large eyes and a hooked beak.

Feet

As parrots, lovebirds have two toes that point forward and two toes that point backward on each foot. This zygodactyl foot helps a lovebird grip his perch securely or climb his cage bars easily, and it also gives him a funny little waddle when he walks across the floor or a tabletop. His feet support his weight evenly. Each toe features a slightly hooked nail that helps a lovebird improve his traction on the perch.

The masked lovebird, Agapornis personata, *is one of the three species of lovebirds that have become popular as pets.*

Coloration

Lovebirds are available in a number of colors. After establishing the lovebird in American aviculture, breeders began to breed uniquely colored birds together to create beautiful mutations. All these colors are based on the lovebirds' normal body feather colors, which are mostly shades of green and blue. These mutations have widened the lovebird color palette, and now owners can choose from shades of blue, green, yellow, and violet, as well as other interesting color combinations, such as white-faced; orange-faced; pied (pied birds have their peach-face coloration diluted or eliminated completely, and their body feathers are various blended shades of greens and

Lovebirds have four toes on each foot—two that point forward and two that point backward.

peach-faced (*Agapornis roseicollis*), the Fischer's (*Agapornis fischeri*), and the masked (*Agapornis personata*)—have become popular pets. The other six species are rare in aviculture due to the low numbers of black-wings (*Agapornis taranta*), black-cheeks (*Agapornis nigrigenis*), Nyasas (*Agapornis lilianae*), and Madagascars (*Agapornis cana*) that have been set up for breeding, despite their having been exported in the 1900s. In the case

blues); creamino (creamino birds have light yellow to white body feathers with red eyes and a blush of light peach-face coloration across the top of the beak); and lutino (lutino birds have bright yellow body feathers with bright red faces and red eyes).

Few of these mutations would be found in nature because unusually colored birds in the wild stand out from their surroundings, making them more visible to predators. In captivity, however, mutations add eye-pleasing colors to already interesting parrot species.

Species

Nine species of lovebirds can be found in the wild, but only three—the

Which Is Better: a Male or a Female?

Like many parrot species, the commonly kept pet species of lovebirds do not show their gender differences outwardly. This makes it very difficult to tell the males from the females without using DNA testing. Some breeders will sex their birds, but most do not take this extra step.

Male lovebirds have the reputation for being easier to tame and less likely to bite than female birds, but female birds may be slightly more likely to talk (although lovebirds are not noted for their talking ability). Purchasing a young hand-fed lovebird, along with patient training and handling by you, the owner, will have a more lasting impact on your bird's tameness than gender will.

of the red-faced lovebird (*Agapornis pullaria*), the birds' preference for using active termite mounds as nesting sites makes them unsuitable for captive breeding, and in the case of the black-collared lovebird (*Agapornis swinderniana*), the birds' diet of fresh figs supplemented with millet makes them difficult to maintain in captivity.

In their native lands, lovebirds can be found on coastal plains, in grasslands and woodlands, in forests, and in river valleys. They eat a wide variety of grasses, grass seeds, grains, fruits, and food crops such as corn and millet. In some places, flocks of lovebirds that feast regularly on food crops are considered pests by the local farmers.

The Lovebird's Temperament and Behavior

What's to love about a lovebird? Lovebird owners find that these small parrots pack a lot of personality into a small package. They provide all the positive benefits of parrot ownership without having to provide room for the full-sized accessories needed by a macaw or cockatoo, which can be a real plus if you're a bird lover who lives in a studio apartment! Your lovebird will entertain you by playing with toys in his cage or on his playgym, and he'll probably seem to sit still only when he's asleep.

Lovebirds are generally bold, outgoing little birds. While this makes

The Lovebird Life Span

With good care, lovebirds can live between 12 and 15 years. You can tell a young lovebird from a mature one by the color of his beak—young birds often have a blackish area underneath their nares (nostrils) that fades as the bird matures.

These small parrots mature quickly and are usually considered mature and ready to breed when they are about six months old. They can breed until they are about seven or eight years of age, but breeding pairs should not be allowed to hatch and raise more than three clutches of eggs a year to give their bodies a chance to rest and to produce healthy chicks in the future.

After about age ten, lovebirds begin to transition into their senior years. They may start to develop molting problems, arthritis, and vision problems. They may need to be fed a diet that is lower in fat to maintain a healthy weight, and they may need to visit the veterinarian more often than they did when they were younger.

Discuss your bird's health with your avian veterinarian as the bird matures so that you can come up with a plan to take care of him in his old age.

Lovebirds come in many vibrant color variations, so you'll be hard pressed to run out of choices.

them amusing companions, it also can get them into trouble because they sometimes forget that they are small parrots. Keep a watchful eye on your lovebird if he decides to interact with your other household pets because he can easily be injured by a rambunctious dog or curious cat. Other household pets, including reptiles and amphibians, can pose a hazard to your lovebird's health because these pets may view your bird as a potential meal and try to consume him.

If you have other birds in your home, you must supervise your lovebird's

interactions with them, too, because lovebirds may be the bully or the bullied, depending on the size and

temperament of your other birds. Lovebirds tend to bully other small parrots, such as parakeets or canaries, while cockatiels may end up bullying your lovebird and keeping him away from food and water bowls in a cage. Larger parrot species probably won't intimidate your lovebird, so be sure to keep an eye on him if he's allowed to interact with larger birds in your home. Many lovebirds don't seem to realize how small they really are, so they need to be protected from themselves as well as from other pets in your home.

If you already have birds in your home, don't try to add a lovebird to the cage of a different bird species. Birds tend to like having their own cages, so let your flock mingle under your watchful eye on playgyms or in other community situations rather than by adding feathered roommates to your birds' cages. If you want to add your lovebird to another cage of lovebirds, purchase a new, larger cage and

The Madagascar Lovebird

Most lovebirds can trace their heritage to central or southern Africa, but one species, the Madagascar lovebird, originated on the island of the same name. In most cases, the lovebirds' native ranges do not overlap, but the habitats of the Fischer's and black-collared lovebirds border on that of the red-faced.

put everyone in it at the same time. This way, none of your birds has the advantage of having lived in the cage first, which can cut down on bullying behavior considerably.

Despite our commonly held vision of lovebirds as a pair of birds snuggled together tightly on a perch, it's not necessary to keep a pair of birds

You don't want to add a new lovebird to a cage containing other bird species or lovebirds who have lived there for awhile.

together to make them content. In fact, if you want to enjoy your lovebird's charming pet qualities, it's better if you keep him as a single pet. Birds who have other birds around them tend to bond with the birds rather than their human companions, while birds kept as single pets rely on their human family to provide them with companionship and entertainment.

Hand-Fed or Parent-Raised: What's the Difference?

When shopping for your lovebird, you may see both "hand-fed" and "parent-raised" birds offered for sale. Chances are that the parent-raised birds will have lower prices than their hand-fed counterparts, so let's look at what you are buying before you adopt your pet.

Hand-fed birds are removed from their nests when they

With seemingly countless options, finding a lovebird you'll love is not a difficult task.

are very young. They are fed and cared for by humans, rather than by their parents, so that the young birds become accustomed to being around people and being handled by them. Hand-fed birds are more trusting of people and are more likely to develop a cuddly personality. Hand-fed birds cost more than parent-raised ones because hand-feeding is a very time-consuming process for the breeder, and it can take several months of around-the-clock care to complete in larger parrot species.

As the term suggests, parent-raised birds are left in their nests to be raised by their parents. They do not become accustomed to being around people from an early age and may be more skittish or more aggressive than a hand-fed bird.

You usually can tell the difference between hand-fed and parent-raised lovebirds when you handle the birds for the first time. The former are more likely to step right onto your hand and want to cuddle with you, while the latter will probably stay away from you and seem fearful.

If you want to keep lovebirds as aviary birds whom you'll admire from a distance, consider buying parent-raised birds. If your goal is to have a playful pet, look at hand-fed birds instead.

Choosing a Lovebird

Determine what you want from your lovebird before you bring him home from the bird store or breeding facility. If you want a pet that will come out of his cage and spend time with you

One Lovebird or Two?

Although many people think of lovebirds as being kept in pairs, single pet birds can be kept successfully. Owners who want a single lovebird should look for a hand-fed baby and be willing to spend time with the bird each day to maintain his tameness. Single lovebirds need regular attention and handling by their owners to ensure that they receive the mental stimulation that another bird would provide.

If you're looking for a less hands-on pet, consider adopting a pair of birds for a large indoor cage or aviary setup.

each day, look for a hand-fed baby lovebird. Be prepared to spend time with your pet every day to ensure that he receives the mental stimulation he needs to be a content pet and to feel like he's part of your family's flock. If you want to admire your bird from afar, purchase a pair of parent-raised lovebirds and enjoy their antics.

Different Lovebird Species

When you visit a bird specialty store or breeding facility, you will likely have three lovebird species from which to choose: the peach-faced, the Fischer's, and the masked. Each has its own unique characteristics, which we'll look at in a bit more detail:

Peach-Faced

The peach-faced lovebird (*Agapornis roseicollis*) is probably the most commonly kept pet lovebird. These lively little acrobats entertain their human families by hanging from or swinging on the toys in their cages. They also enjoy flying in quick, straight flights, so try to provide your pet lovebird with a large rectangular cage to give him a chance to stretch his wings a bit each day. Single peach-faced lovebirds can become devoted pets if their owners give them consistent daily attention.

Although you often can't tell male lovebirds from females, female peach-faced lovebirds have one common behavior that often gives them away: They love to shred paper and tuck it into their rump feathers before flying to a chosen nesting site. If your pet suddenly starts tucking torn paper or other materials into its rump feathers, you probably have a female lovebird.

More than a dozen color mutations of the peach-faced lovebird have been developed, so don't be surprised to see a rainbow of birds available for purchase at your bird store or from a breeder.

For all their positive qualities, peach-faced lovebirds are also considered among the most aggressive of lovebird species. They will bully other small birds in an aviary setting, so it's best not to house them with other bird species for the safety of all the feathered pets in your home.

Fischer's

The Fischer's lovebird (*Agapornis fischeri*) is also an active little bird. This species is considered an eye-ring lovebird because of the circle of bare skin around the bird's eyes. The Fischer's is a hardy little bird who enjoys spending time with his owners. These energetic birds are noted for their robust natures. Breeders have developed several color mutations in Fischer's lovebirds, so you may have a few colors from which to choose.

The main drawback of the Fischer's is that this bird has a more piercing call than other lovebird species. If noise is a concern for you, consider a different lovebird species. Look for hand-fed Fischer's lovebirds because parent-raised chicks can be a bit nervous around people.

Masked

The masked lovebird (*Agapornis personata*) also is considered an eye-ring lovebird species. They are affectionate little parrots who enjoy amusing their owners with their playful antics. Breeders have developed about a half-dozen color mutations of masked lovebirds.

Like their peach-faced cousins, female masked lovebirds have a behavior that gives them away in a pet setting. Female masked lovebirds carry nesting materials around in their beaks, so if your pet suddenly starts carrying small items around, chances are she's a female in search of a nest site.

Masked lovebirds also can be aggressive, so try to find a hand-fed bird when selecting a pet.

Others

The other six lovebird species—the Nyasa, the Madagascar, the black-winged, the black-cheeked, the red-faced, and the black-collared—are difficult to find as pets in the United States.

Lovebirds

Are Lovebirds Good Pets for Children?

Lovebirds have all the personality of larger parrot species in a smaller package. This smaller size makes them easier for both children and adults to handle, and it makes them more approachable as a family pet than larger parrot species might be.

With proper supervision from parents, lovebirds can be suitable pets for families. Children ages eight and older can help their parents take part in the bird's daily care and training, while younger children can take part in the bird's caretaking by helping choose healthy foods and safe toys for him during shopping trips to the supermarket and pet store.

With all their charming qualities, lovebirds have a lot to offer. One thing they don't do well is learn to talk. Over the years, only a few reports have surfaced of talking lovebirds, and these few talking birds seemed to master only a few words. If you want a small parrot who can learn to talk easily, consider a parakeet instead of a lovebird (keeping in mind that no bird is guaranteed to talk). Your lovebird will probably chatter or twitter at you throughout the day, but he isn't likely to speak clearly enough for you to impress your family and friends.

The lovebird's lively nature makes him a good candidate for trick training, and his clever mind will learn new things quickly. Make short trick training sessions a part of your bird's daily routine and you soon may have a little feathered star on your hands. These daily training sessions also will help your pet burn off some of his seemingly endless supply of energy, which will make him easier to handle and will create a happier relationship between you and your bird. We'll look at trick training in more detail in Chapter 6.

Lovebirds are clever and lively, and so are naturals at learning tricks.

Hand-fed young lovebirds mature into fun-loving little pets with few behavior problems if they are handled each day to maintain their pet qualities. If they are left alone in their cages, however, they may become aggressive and may be reluctant to come out to play with you. These cage-bound birds (birds who spend too much time alone in their cages) also may bite your hand when you try to take them out. This can set the stage for a potentially endless cycle of poor lovebird behavior. Your bird needs to be taken out of his cage and handled so that you can interact with him, but if he bites you, you'll be less likely to want him out of his cage. Prevent this problem from happening by taking a little time each day to play with and handle your pet. Daily handling ensures that your pet maintains his tameness, and it also offers him a chance to check out the pockets of your shirt or cuddle up next to your neck as you two spend time together.

A common behavior that new lovebird owners need to know about is his love of chewing. Lovebirds will shred their cage tray liner if they have access to it, and they will shred any other paper they can get their beaks on! They also will chew their cage perches, their cage covers, the magazines on your coffee table, the coffee table itself, and anything else chewable they can find, whether it's a bird toy or not. Provide plenty of safe, chewable toys for your lovebird so that he can do what comes naturally without destroying valuable documents, precious antique furniture, or other important items in your home.

19

Above all, your lovebird will love to play and have fun!

Chapter 2

The Stuff of

Everyday Life

Before bringing your lovebird home, you'll need to have a few supplies on hand to make your new pet feel safe and comfortable. These include a cage with appropriately sized perches, two sets of food and water bowls, a cuttlebone or mineral block, some toys, a bird bathtub, and grooming supplies. You also may want a playgym to give your pet a place to play outside his cage; a seed catcher that fits around the cage to contain seed hulls, molted feathers, and other birdie debris; and a cage cover, although a clean sheet or bath towel free of holes and frayed spots will work just as well.

Your Lovebird's Home

The Cage

The most important accessory your lovebird will need is a safe and secure cage. He requires a cage in which he feels comfortable, and he must be safe and secure inside of it. Because lovebirds are active little parrots, choose a cage that allows your pet ample opportunities to fly and climb.

The cage must be large enough to accommodate your lovebird, his food and water bowls, his toys, and a small bird bathtub for his regular baths. Also, allow space for a swing near the top of the cage because swings are very popular toys with many lovebirds.

Don't shortchange the space in your cage because your pet will be spending a fair amount of time in it. Even with ample out-of-cage time, he'll still be inside of it while you're away from home at school or work during the day, so he'll need some room to move around without feeling cramped.

An ideal cage size for a single lovebird is 36 inches by 20 inches by 20 inches (91 cm by 51 cm by 51 cm, but bigger is always better. For the health and well-being of your bird, buy the largest cage you can afford. Your lovebird has a potential life span of 12 years, and he should have a comfortable home in which to live during that time. Larger cages provide more flying and playing room; the larger size gives

him a more interesting environment and can help to improve his quality of life. Owners of Fischer's lovebirds especially should look for spacious cages for their pets. These acrobatic little clowns seem to need more room to climb and play than other lovebird species.

Acrylic or Wire?

Although you may be tempted by plastic, bamboo, or wooden cages, none of them is a suitable home for your lovebird. Lovebirds and other parrots spend a lot of time chewing each day, and their strong beaks make quick work of these cages. For your pet's safety, house him in a wire or acrylic cage.

Most people are accustomed to the traditional wire bird cage, but acrylic cages are another housing option.

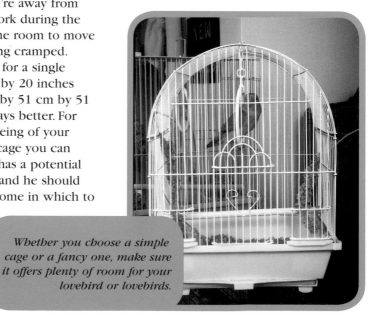

Whether you choose a simple cage or a fancy one, make sure it offers plenty of room for your lovebird or lovebirds.

Acrylic cages first came on the market in the early 1990s, and their main selling point is the ease of cleanup, along with a slightly better view of your pet bird through the clear acrylic cage as opposed to traditional wire bars.

Acrylic cages are better than their wire counterparts at containing bird debris, such as seed hulls or molted feathers, and this small factor may make birdkeeping easier and more enjoyable for you. Acrylic cages also may be easier to clean than wire cages because they can be cleaned simply by wiping the sides inside and out with a damp towel and by changing the tray liner daily.

If you purchase an acrylic cage for your lovebird, make sure that it has numerous ventilation holes drilled in its walls to allow for adequate air circulation. Keep your lovebird out of direct sunlight if he lives in an acrylic cage because it can get warm rather quickly and your bird could become overheated. Give your pet several ladders between his perches because the smooth sides of an acrylic cage don't offer the same climbing opportunities that a pet bird has in a wire cage.

If you're purchasing a wire cage, the bar spacing should measure 3/8 inch (9½ mm), and the cage should feature horizontal bars for climbing in addition to the main vertical cage bars.

The Cage Tray

Whether made of acrylic or wire, the cage should have a slide-out tray to

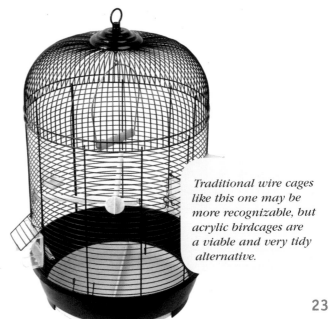

Traditional wire cages like this one may be more recognizable, but acrylic birdcages are a viable and very tidy alternative.

23

catch debris and a grille to keep your pet out of the tray itself. The cage tray should slide out easily for daily cleaning, and it should be of a shape that's easy to line with paper, such as a rectangle. Round or oddly shaped cages are a bit more difficult to clean and maintain because the trays aren't as easy to line with newspaper, paper towels, or used printer paper. Make it easy on yourself and purchase a rectangular cage.

Ground walnut shells, cat litter, and wood shavings are not appropriate choices to put in your bird's cage tray. He could ingest any of them, which could cause intestinal problems, and they don't do a good job of containing bird debris. You're much better off using a simple paper liner, such as black-and-white newspaper or used paper, in your bird's cage tray.

When You're Away, Your Bird Will Play

Keeping your lovebird entertained while you're away at work or school is a fairly simple thing to do. First, make sure that he has ample supplies of his favorite pellets and access to clean drinking water. You also can offer him fresh vegetables and fruits if you live in a temperate climate where food does not spoil quickly at room temperature.

Next, give him interesting toys to play with and enough room to move about his cage during playtime. Remove any toys that look worn or frayed so that your pet doesn't injure himself while you're out of the house. Also, trim your bird's nails regularly to prevent injury.

Finally, consider leaving a radio or television on for your bird. This will keep your house from seeming too quiet, which in turn will help to reduce your bird's stress level. In the wild, quiet surroundings can signal danger, and even though your lovebird isn't a wild animal, he still may react instinctively to a too-quiet environment by going into a stressful fight-or-flight mindset.

The Cage Door

The cage door is another important feature. The door should open wide enough to allow you to put your hand in and out of the cage easily, and it also should be able to accommodate your bird's food and water bowls, along with his bathtub. The door must close securely enough to keep your bird inside the cage, but it should open easily for you from the outside.

Cage door choices include drawbridge-style doors that open from the top and form a porch for the bird to play on, guillotine-style doors that slide open from the bottom, and side-opening doors that can be hooked out of the way to allow easy access to the inside of the cage. Of these three, the guillotine-style door is probably the least desirable. Some birds have been injured by the cage door sliding down on them unexpectedly, so try to steer clear of this door when choosing your pet's cage.

Location, Location, Location

Where you place your lovebird's cage in your home is important. Select a spot in your home that's in the normal traffic flow, such as the family room. Place your lovebird's cage so that he has a solid wall behind him, rather than having the cage sit in the middle of the room or far enough away from a wall that a family member or pet could easily get behind the cage. Your bird will feel more secure if he has a solid wall behind him because he won't have to worry about something or

Lining your birdcage with something simple like newspaper is easier and sometimes safer than using fancier liner materials.

someone sneaking up on him from behind.

Don't place your bird's cage directly in a window or patio door. Areas around windows and doors can become too hot or too cold, and neither of these situations is good for your bird. Don't set up your bird's cage in a bathroom or kitchen, either—these rooms are subject to temperature changes that aren't good for your bird, and chemical cleaning products frequently used in these rooms may give off harmful fumes.

Set up the cage before you bring your lovebird home. Joining your family will be a stressful event for him (at least until he settles into the routine

of your home). You don't want to add to the stress by waiting until the last minute to decide where to place his cage. Having the cage already set up allows your lovebird to begin settling in as soon as you put him in his new home.

Adding the Accessories

Perches

Once you have your lovebird's cage set up, it's time to start furnishing his new home. Perches are particularly vital to your pet's comfort. Without them, your bird will have nowhere to sit in his home

Your lovebird will feel safer with a wall close behind or forming at least one wall of his cage.

Household Fumes

Because your lovebird has a delicate respiratory system, you must be careful about the types of cleaning products you use in your home. Many products, including household cleaners, air fresheners, paints, glues, cosmetics, and even some kitchen appliances, produce fumes that can harm your pet.

One item that new bird owners need to be aware of is nonstick cookware. Under normal conditions, this product makes cleanup after cooking easy without harming your bird's health. However, if it is allowed to overheat, the nonstick surface produces fumes that can kill pet birds. Replace your nonstick cookware with stainless steel or other bird-safe products.

To keep your pet safe from harm, use chemicals sparingly in your home, and try to be as far away from your bird's cage as possible when you do so. You also might want to investigate some "green," or natural, cleaning products, such as baking soda, vinegar, lemon juice, and mineral oil, to help keep your home fume free.

Not surprisingly, your lovebird will need a few perches in his cage, but they should all be small enough for his toes to curl around them comfortably.

except on the cage floor, which isn't an ideal situation. Your bird needs to be able to sit in two or three locations, and perches provide the best way for him to do this.

Place perches in your bird's cage on opposite ends so that he can fly from end to end. Locate his food and water bowls near a perch so that he can easily eat or drink, and place one perch a little higher than the rest in the cage so that he has a secure sleeping spot at night.

In addition to the traditional wooden dowel perches that come with many birdcage kits, perch materials can include concrete, rope, or natural woods, such as manzanita. Concrete perches are designed to help keep a bird's nails and beak trimmed, but they may cause some birds to develop sore feet, so check your bird's feet for signs of soreness if you provide a concrete perch. Rope perches provide a softer surface and some play value, but they can also become frayed if your bird is a determined chewer. Check rope perches regularly for signs of wear, and replace them if they become frayed or soiled. Manzanita perches provide a challenge to the most determined chewers in the bird world, so consider offering a manzanita perch if you notice your lovebird easily chews through his wooden dowel perches.

Try to offer your bird different perching surfaces and diameters when setting up his cage. The recommended perch diameter for a lovebird is 1/2 inch (1 cm), so select perches with that diameter or a little larger when setting up the cage. Having a slightly larger perch diameter will assist your bird in stretching his foot muscles, which helps to keep his feet healthier than if he is forced to use perches that are all the same size.

Sandpaper Perch Covers

You may think that you're doing your lovebird a favor by purchasing some sandpaper perch covers to help to keep his nails trimmed, but these items actually may do more harm than good. Your lovebird's nails likely won't grow long enough for the perch cover to have any effect on them, and the rough surface of the sandpaper may cause

Keep in mind that love-birds love to chew. Wooden dowel or rope perches need to be changed when showing signs of wear.

Grit

your bird to develop foot sores, so they are best left out of your bird's cage.

Dishing Out the Food and Water

Your lovebird's food and water bowls are also very important cage accessories. These can be either sturdy plastic bowls that attach to the cage with metal hooks or ceramic dishes that sit on the cage floor. You'll need to have at least two sets of bowls on hand so that you can easily provide your pet with fresh food and water in the morning and in the evening. If possible, keep more than two sets of bowls—this will make feeding and watering your pet easier because you'll have a clean set of bowls available at mealtime. Wash the bowls with hot, soapy water and rinse them thoroughly before placing them in your bird's cage.

When placing the food and water bowls in your lovebird's cage, locate them so that they are not directly underneath his primary perching spot. This will help the food and water in them stay cleaner because your bird won't be likely to eliminate in them. Place the bowls near a perch so that your bird can eat and drink comfortably.

In addition to food and water bowls, your lovebird will benefit from having a cuttlebone or mineral block placed in his cage. A cuttlebone is the shell of a marine animal called a cuttlefish, and it supplies calcium and other minerals your bird needs to maintain his health. Mineral blocks are available in different shapes, sizes, and flavors, and as the name implies, provide important minerals for your lovebird. Your lovebird will likely chew through his cuttlebone or mineral

Your lovebird will need at least one set of food and water dishes containing fresh food and drink in his cage at all times.

Why Your Lovebird Should Be a Family Pet

Although your child may beg and plead to have a lovebird as her own personal pet, it's better for both the bird and your family to keep him as a family pet. Children may think they're up for the daily care and maintenance of a pet at first, but when the novelty wears off, the pet is still there, waiting to be cared for.

When the daily bird care chores fall to you, don't threaten your child into caring for the bird. Don't say that you're going to give the bird away or get rid of him, because those statements show a child that a pet is a disposable commodity rather than another living creature to be appreciated and loved.

Keep your lovebird's cage in the family room or another part of the house where your family gathers regularly. This will help him feel like part of the flock/family, and it will ensure that he is cared for each day. Birds who end up living in their young owners' rooms may feel isolated from the rest of the household, and they may not be cared for each day because their cages are not in the main living area.

By making the bird a family pet, you're helping your child learn responsibility. She can take over more day-to-day care of the bird as she matures, but you will always be there to back your child up so that your lovebird isn't neglected. By doing this, your child will see what it takes to care for a pet, and you all will grow from the experience.

Ideally, bird ownership is a commitment that lasts the lifetime of the bird, which in the case of a lovebird can be 12 to 15 years or more. In 12 years, your child may go from elementary school to college, which means that your lovebird will help to ease the transition to an "empty nest" for you.

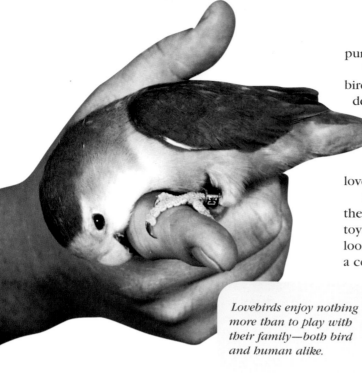

Lovebirds enjoy nothing more than to play with their family—both bird and human alike.

purchase replacements.

When choosing toys for your bird, be sure to consider only those designed for small parrots. Lovebirds could injure themselves if they try to play with toys meant for Amazons or cockatoos, so look for toys that are designed for lovebirds, budgies, or cockatiels.

Look at the fasteners that attach the toy to the cage, and try to select toys with quick-link fasteners. These look like a capital "C" that closes into a complete link with a small threaded section that's attached to the bottom of the "C." These are safer for pet birds than split-ring fasteners, snap locks, or other hooks because playful birds are less likely to catch a toe or beak in a quick link.

Other safety concerns to be aware of include:

- jingle-type bells (a bird's toe can become trapped in the small opening)

- ring toys (a bird can become caught in the rings)

- lead-weighted toys (these can be cracked open, exposing the lead that a bird may chew on)

- brittle plastic toys (these can shatter if a bird breaks them with his beak)

Lovebirds are great chewers, so purchase several chew toys for your bird to enjoy. Look for toys made from untreated, unpainted wood, cotton rope, and vegetable-tanned leather. Inspect your bird's toys daily once

block rather quickly, so be sure to have a replacement on hand.

Lovebirds Love to Play

Toys are one of the most enjoyable cage accessories for both birds and owners. Your lovebird will probably spend a lot of time playing, so it's important for him to have interesting and safe toys in his cage.

When you walk down the bird toy aisle at your local pet supply store, you may feel a little overwhelmed by the variety. Your bird's breeder or the pet store staff can make some recommendations as to which types of toys lovebirds enjoy, and you'll soon learn which toys your bird likes when it comes time to he begins playing with them, and promptly replace any that are worn to provide him with maximum chewing fun.

Many lovebirds enjoy swings, so you may want to purchase one for your bird. If you do, include enough space for the swing in his cage so that he will be able to enjoy his new home in comfort.

Bathtime Is Fun Time

In addition to playing in his cage, your lovebird will enjoy regular baths in his home. Most lovebirds are enthusiastic bathers, so it won't take much encouragement from you to get your bird to take a dip in his bird bathtub. Provide about 1/2 inch (1 cm) of lukewarm water in the bathtub early in the day so that your pet has an opportunity to dry and preen his feathers before bedtime.

If you don't want to purchase a bird bathtub for your lovebird, mist him under a sink faucet daily with lukewarm water or spray him with a mister bottle that's used just for bird baths. Unless they've gotten themselves into something really oily, pet birds just need a little lukewarm water for bathing—they don't need special shampoos or conditioning sprays under normal circumstances.

Looking Good

Although he'll take care of a lot of routine grooming himself, your lovebird will need to have his wings and nails trimmed regularly to keep him safe.

Your grooming supplies will include a small washcloth or towel, a set of nail clippers, a nail file, a vial of styptic powder, a pair of needle-nosed pliers, and a pair of scissors. While we'll talk about how to use all this equipment in Chapter 4, this list is being provided here so that you'll know what to put

There are all sorts of different toys out there for lovebirds to play with, so let your pets try out different kinds so they never get bored.

Homemade Bird Toys

Not all bird toys have to come from the pet supply store. Some safe and entertaining bird toys can be made at home, and making the toys is another way you can involve your children in caring for your lovebird.

Some toys are surprisingly simple. Cut up an empty paper towel roll into about 2-inch-long (5-cm) sections, then cut the sections along one side to make the roll into a "C" and offer them to your lovebird. Your bird will enjoy chewing up the thin cardboard, and splitting the side of the roll ensures that he won't become a prisoner of this toy if he happens to toss a section over his head during playtime.

You can make another simple toy by stringing uncooked pasta or unsweetened breakfast cereal on a clean piece of cotton string or vegetable-tanned leather. Your lovebird will enjoy destroying the pasta or cereal, and he won't be harmed if he eats a little along the way. You can adapt this idea during the holidays by making a lovebird-sized garland of popcorn and cranberries (or whatever fresh fruits your bird enjoys) for him to play with as you decorate the rest of your house.

You also can entertain your bird by hiding sliced grapes or small pieces of nuts under a paper muffin cup. Send your bird on a scavenger hunt around his playgym this way, or just keep giving him hidden treats as he discovers what's under the cup.

on your shopping list.

Consider keeping all of your grooming supplies in a plastic box so that they will be easily found when it's time to groom your pet. If you don't want to keep them in a box, you can place them on a shelf near your pet's cage so that they are easily accessible.

Playgyms for Playtime

As mentioned earlier, lovebirds love to play, so you may want to purchase a playgym for your bird. Some bird cages have the option of having the cage top open into a playgym, or the playgym can be a separate, free-standing structure. In either case, these gyms allow a lovebird to climb, play, and swing in a bird-safe area outside his cage. They can be as simple or as complex as you choose—the only restrictions are your imagination and budget.

If you're handy with tools, you can even build your own playgym for your bird. Use untreated lumber and zinc-free fasteners in your project to ensure your pet's safety. You can find plans online or by consulting bird specialty magazines.

Other Accessories

Two other accessories you may want to consider for your lovebird are a seed catcher and a cage cover. The seed catcher helps to contain discarded food, old feathers, and other debris that fall out of your bird's cage. Without a seed catcher, these items end up on the floor, which means you'll either be vacuuming frequently or you'll have a messy floor.

The first seed catchers were simple tubes made out of elasticized cloth, and they attached to the bird cage by being pulled over them and bunched up around the bottom of the cage. Although this style of seed catcher is still around, seed containment has taken on a life of its own. In fact, cage manufacturers have developed several ways to contain the mess, including plastic or glass sheets that slide in around the outside of the cage bottom and corral the mess, and more elaborate metal aprons that flare out underneath the cage and contain the debris inside.

A cage cover can help your lovebird settle in at bedtime. Some birds seem to prefer the darkness the cover provides, especially if the bird stays in the family room or some other part of the house that will still have lights on after the bird has gone to sleep for the night.

You can purchase a cage cover or use an old sheet, towel, or blanket. Whichever type of cover you choose, be sure that it is clean and free of holes before placing it over your bird's cage.

Because lovebirds are such noted chewers, your bird will probably put some holes in his cage cover fairly quickly. Some birds seem to find

You'll need to bathe or at least mist your bird in lukewarm water to keep him clean, but avoid using any conditioners or shampoos—your bird doesn't need them.

Playgyms and other fun toys will become a popular attraction in your birdcage, so try to provide plenty of different things for your birds to do.

droppings and other debris.

Wash and scrub your pet's cage weekly. Remove your lovebird and all his accessories, such as bowls, toys, and perches, from the cage before beginning to wash it. (Put your lovebird into a small travel cage or set him on his playgym with appropriate supervision during cage cleaning time.) Also, use a wet paper towel to remove any food that's stuck to the cage bars.

Put the empty cage into your bathroom shower and set the shower temperature to hot. Hot water will loosen any stuck-on food that didn't come off when you wiped the

comfort in chewing on their covers, while others seem to want to observe their family's activities by nibbling a few peepholes in it. Keep an eye on the condition of your bird's cage cover, and replace it when it has too many holes in it to be effective.

Keeping the Cage Clean

Cage cleaning is an important part of lovebird care. A clean cage helps your pet stay healthy and provides him with an interesting, safe environment.

As part of your daily routine, change the food and water bowls in the enclosure and provide fresh food and water in clean dishes. Change the cage paper daily, too, to remove your pet's

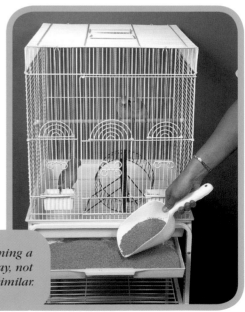

Slide-out trays make cage cleaning a snap, but use only paper in the tray, not a corn cob or something similar.

bars with a wet paper towel. Use a toothbrush or a small scrub brush to loosen any remaining food or droppings, then rinse the cage with more hot water.

After the cage is clean, spray it with a bird-safe disinfectant that's recommended for cages. Follow the

Your Bird's Travel Carrier

In addition to your lovebird's regular cage, he will need to have a small travel carrier for trips to the veterinarian's office. The carrier also works well as your bird's temporary shelter while you give his cage its weekly cleaning and disinfection.

Some lovebirds take to their carriers immediately. Their natural curiosity overcomes any fear they might have, and they walk right in and make themselves comfortable. If your lovebird is a bit shy around his carrier, though, he may need a step-by-step introduction to it. Here's how to do it.

1. First, set up the carrier near your bird's usual cage. Give him two or three days to get adjusted to it from a distance, then begin moving it closer to his cage.
2. After about a week, your lovebird should be comfortable with the sight of his carrier. Take him out of his cage and place him in the carrier with the door open. Praise him for staying in it, even if it's just for a moment. Place him in the carrier several times a day to get him used to being in there.
3. After your bird seems comfortable staying in the carrier with the door open, try closing the door. Praise your bird for staying there with the door closed. Let him out immediately if he seems distressed by the closed door. If he isn't bothered, see if he will stay inside for a few minutes. Repeat the process several times a day until your bird seems comfortable being in the carrier.
4. Once your bird is comfortable inside the carrier, place him and the carrier inside your car and close the door. If he seems comfortable inside the car, take him around the block for a short car ride. If he's uncomfortable, open the door and remove him and his carrier. Reassure him that all is well and that he's being a good bird.

Work with your bird a little each day until he seems comfortable having his carrier inside your car, then take him on a short car ride to see how he does. Most birds enjoy car travel, but some do get carsick, so it's best to work with your lovebird early on to help him enjoy car rides as much as possible.

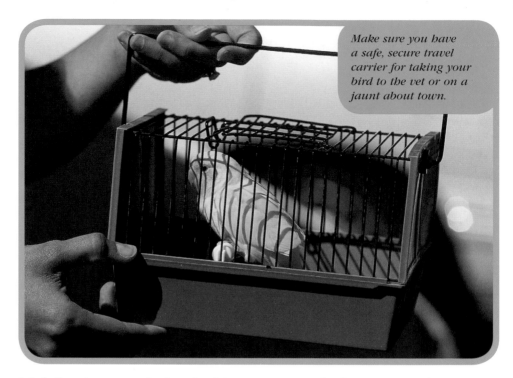

Make sure you have a safe, secure travel carrier for taking your bird to the vet or on a jaunt about town.

label directions as to the length of time the disinfectant needs to stay on the cage to be effective. After disinfecting, rinse the cage thoroughly to remove any traces of the chemicals. Let the cage air-dry while you clean the perches and inspect your lovebird's toys for signs of wear.

Scrape and sand wooden, ceramic, or plastic perches to remove any stuck-on droppings or food. Wash and dry them thoroughly before returning them to the cage. Check rope perches for signs of fraying, and clean them according to the manufacturer's instructions.

Change the toys in your lovebird's cage to keep his environment interesting. Throw out toys that are worn or broken to ensure that your pet doesn't hurt himself during playtime.

Replace the perches and other cage accessories when the cage is completely dry, and return your bird to his clean home.

Cleanup Schedule

Daily: Change cage paper, replace food and water, and inspect toys and perches for signs of wear. Weekly: Wash and disinfect cage and perches, change toys, and replace worn perches.

A Bird-Proofed Home

To help to protect your lovebird from harm, you'll need to bird-proof your home. Lovebirds are naturally curious creatures, and your pet needs your help to channel this curiosity into safe behaviors.

Here's a room-by-room look at some things you'll need to be aware of before your lovebird explores your home:

The *bathroom* is a place many lovebirds may find attractive, especially because of all the mirrors and shiny chrome fixtures. Watch your bird around open toilet bowls and full sinks, keep electrical cords out of reach of his beak, and be careful using chemicals or cosmetics with him in the room because some products create harmful fumes.

The *kitchen* is a place lovebirds could come to love quickly because this is where all the food is! If your lovebird is in your kitchen, watch for open appliances, hot pots and pans, and unattended foods that can be hazardous to your bird's health (e.g., chocolate, rhubarb, avocado).

The *living room* or *family room* is a likely lovebird hangout because this is probably where your family spends a lot of time, and lovebirds hate to miss out on any of the action! When your bird is out of his cage in these rooms, watch that he doesn't run under couch cushions or pillows or chew on your game console's electrical cords. Also, keep an eye on your pet if you have anything tempting on your coffee table, from a stained glass lamp shade to an ashtray full of cigarette butts, because your lovebird may want to taste-test the items.

No matter what room you're in, keep an eye on your bird at all times. Hide the room's electrical cords in PVC piping or cord containers designed to conceal wiring in home theaters so that your bird won't chew on them. Put away craft or sewing projects so that he doesn't come into contact with sharp needles, paints, or glues. Make sure that ceiling fans are turned off before your bird comes out of his cage so that he isn't injured by the fan blades, and check all open doors and windows to ensure that their screens are secure.

Chapter 3

Eating Well

Now that you know what items your lovebird will need to live comfortably in your home, it's time to discuss his diet. Diet and nutrition are important parts of your lovebird's daily routine because most of these little parrots love to eat. (You can use this love of food to train your lovebird, which we'll discuss in detail in Chapter 6.)

eeding a good-quality diet also helps to protect your pet's health, which we'll discuss in depth in Chapter 5. For now, it's important to know that feeding a quality diet helps to prevent health problems such as potentially life-threatening infections and less serious issues such as feather problems and flaky skin.

What Goes in the Food Bowl

To maintain his health, your lovebird needs to eat a wide variety of nutrients each day, including proteins, carbohydrates, fats, vitamins, and minerals. All this probably sounds complicated, but it's actually pretty easy. Let's look at what each nutrient provides your bird and how you can offer it to him each day.

Proteins

A lovebird needs proteins to grow, maintain good health, and reproduce.

Proteins are made up of amino acids, which a bird's body cannot make on its own. Good protein sources include nuts, beans, eggs, meats, and dairy products.

Carbohydrates

Carbs give a lovebird's body fuel to keep going. They can be broken down into starches and simple sugars, and they are the only energy source that a bird's brain uses. Good carbohydrate sources include vegetables, fruits, and cereals.

Fats

Fats help a lovebird's body store energy, and they provide insulation for the body against the cold. Good fat sources include nuts, seeds, and dairy products. Owners of Abyssinian lovebirds, take note: Your bird has a higher fat requirement than other lovebird species, so be sure to provide him with

Not just seed eaters as they once were assumed to be, lovebirds young and old need many different aspects to their diet to be as healthy as possible.

Vitamins

A lovebird needs several essential vitamins to maintain his health. One of the most important of these is vitamin A. Vitamin A helps to ward off infections, and it is available in dark green or dark orange vegetables, such as broccoli, sweet potatoes, carrots, spinach, and dandelion greens (the ones you buy at the supermarket, not the ones in your yard that could be contaminated with weed killers or other chemicals).

Other vitamin-rich foods in your lovebird's diet can include sunflower and safflower seeds, oats, milo, eggs, wheat germ, cabbage, Brussels sprouts, cauliflower, and peanuts.

Items You Should Not Feed Your Bird

Never feed the following items to a lovebird because they have the potential to harm his health:

- alcohol
- avocado
- candy and other sugary snack foods
- chocolate
- mushrooms
- onions
- rhubarb
- salty foods, such as potato chips, pretzels, or french fries
- seeds or pits from fruits, including apples, cherries, pears, peaches, and plums
- spoiled produce

a few sunflower seeds every other day or so to meet his additional fat needs.

Eating Well

Lovebirds in nature eat many different types of plants and fruits, which is good reason to offer your pet lovebirds an array of foods as well.

Minerals

Minerals are an important part of a lovebird's diet because they help to keep a bird's cells, nerves, and muscles functioning normally. Good sources of minerals include pumpkin seeds, bananas, carrots, nuts, and peanuts. A supplemental mineral block in your lovebird's cage also can provide some of these vital nutrients.

Discuss your lovebird's diet with your avian veterinarian to ensure that your bird is receiving all the nutrients he needs to maintain his health.

What Wild Lovebirds Eat

In their native habitats, lovebirds eat a wide variety of plant foods, including tree and grass seeds; berries; food crops such as rice, corn, or millet; and fruits such as figs. Five lovebird species—the Fischer's, the masked, the Nyasa, the Madagascar, and the red-faced—are considered ground-feeding parrots, which means that they spend part of their day on the ground searching for

Fruits and vegetables can be a staple of your lovebird's diet. They're healthy, natural, and tasty.

Why Your Bird Needs Water

In addition to fresh, nutritious food, your lovebird must have access to clean, fresh water at all times. Although he'll probably try to bathe in his water bowl from time to time, he needs to be able to drink from it, too. Birds need water to digest their food properly and to maintain their health. Water moves nutrients through a bird's body, and it also removes waste products.

Your lovebird must have access to clean, fresh water each day. If you notice that your bird's water bowl is often fouled by droppings or discarded food, move it to another location in the cage. Fouled or contaminated water provides a good place for bacteria to grow, and unclean water can cause health problems for your bird if he drinks it.

If there's no place you can put the water bowl to prevent it from being fouled, or if your lovebird is bathing in his water bowl more than he is drinking from it, offer his drinking water in a water bottle like the ones used for hamsters and guinea pigs. As you transition your bird to using a water bottle, make sure that he knows how to drink from the water bottle before you remove his water bowl permanently.

Lovebirds are well known in the pet bird world for being big drinkers, so check your bird's water bowl or bottle several times a day to ensure that he has enough to drink.

Encouraging a Finicky Eater

Although most lovebirds readily dive into their food bowls, some birds can be finicky eaters. If your pet turns up his beak at new foods, you may have to try a few tricks to encourage him to eat.

One way to do this is to pretend you're eating the new food item. The more you act excited and interested in the food, and the more you seem to enjoy "eating" it, the better. Birds love drama, so the more enthusiastic your acting is, the better the chance that your lovebird will find it hard to resist the new food.

If another bird in your home already eats the food you want your lovebird to try, use that bird to demonstrate his interest in the food in a "monkey see, monkey do" approach. Set up your lovebird's cage where he can see the other bird enjoying the new food. In no time, both birds should be enjoying the new food with gusto.

Whether you're trying to introduce it yourself or you're having another bird in your home help to get your lovebird to try new foods, please don't withhold familiar food from your lovebird's bowl during new food introductions. Don't starve your bird either. Provide him with both old favorites and new foods to ensure that he eats the familiar foods while experimenting with new tastes.

Don't be discouraged if your lovebird doesn't dive right in to a new food. Some birds have to become adjusted to new foods, while others will try anything new. Offer new foods regularly and praise your pet when you see him eating them. Before you know it, your once-finicky bird will be eager to try new things.

food, and they also eat a lot of their food on the ground as opposed to eating in trees as some other above-ground-feeding parrots do. The black-winged, the black-collared, the peach-faced, and the black-cheeked lovebirds are considered above-ground-feeding parrots.

In farming areas, flocks of lovebirds can descend on the fields at harvest time and consume the crops. Their love of food crops and fruits causes some wild birds to be destroyed each year because farmers in Africa and Madagascar consider them agricultural pests. Lovebirds have been shown to damage up to 30 percent of a region's crops at harvest time.

In the case of two lovebird species, this love of food crops has placed them on an at-risk list with a major conservation organization. According to the International Union for the Conservation of Nature and Natural

Supplements

Most lovebirds have healthy appetites and eat a wide enough variety of foods that they probably won't need to have supplements added to their diets. Discuss your bird's diet with your avian veterinarian and add supplements only if she thinks it's a good idea.

One thing you don't want to do is add vitamins or any other substance to your bird's water bowl or bottle. Adding vitamins to the water changes the taste and may make your bird less likely to drink, and contaminate it, encouraging bacteria to grow, which can cause your bird to become ill.

Another item you won't need to add to your lovebird's diet is grit. Grit is made up of small stones and coarse sand. Birdkeepers used to offer it to pet birds to help their crops (a muscular internal organ that aids in digestion) grind up their food.

We now know that most pet birds (except pigeons and doves) don't need grit and that it actually is more harmful than helpful. Birds offered grit will often consume too much of it, which results in impacted or overly full crops. This condition requires veterinary attention for the bird to recover.

Resources (IUCN), the Nyasa lovebird is considered "nearly threatened," and the black-cheeked lovebird is considered "vulnerable." In both cases, the birds' status as pest species is part of the reason they have been listed as an at-risk species. The other seven lovebird species are considered "not threatened" at this time by the IUCN.

A lovebird's diet in the wild can affect its popularity as a pet species, too. A dependence upon fresh figs as a primary food source is one of the reasons the black-collared lovebird didn't catch on as a pet species. Although other lovebird species such as the red-faced and the Abyssinian favor figs, the diet of the black-collared lovebird diet is so dependent upon fresh figs that no satisfactory substitute exists in captivity.

Picking the Proper Diet

The pet supply store offers bird owners several food choices. If you're new to the world of birdkeeping, you're probably wondering which type of food your lovebird needs: seeds or pellets.

For many years, pet birds subsisted on seed-only diets. My childhood parakeet, Charlie, was one of those birds. We fed him a parakeet seed mix from the pet store because that's what we thought was best for him, and that's what he ate for the five years we had him. We never thought to offer him fresh foods because the thinking in the 1960s was "birds eat seed."

My next parrot, an African grey named Sindbad, fared a little better at

The days of seed-only diets are over, but that doesn't mean they don't have their place as one of the main components of your lovebird's diet.

Make sure your lovebird always has fresh food. If there is waste in the food dish, your pet could become very sick.

mealtime after I adopted her as an adult bird in the late 1980s. In addition to seeds (something that was a familiar staple in her previous home), she could choose from pellets, fresh fruits, fresh vegetables, cheddar cheese cubes, walnuts, peanuts, almonds, and healthy people foods such as unsweetened cereals, corn bread, whole wheat crackers, rice cakes, and unsalted pretzels during the ten years I had her. Some of my friends claimed the bird ate better than I did, and they were right!

The diets fed to my two pet birds illustrate how little people knew about their needs more than 40 years ago and how far feeding pet birds has come today. What began as one extreme of seed-only diets in the 1950s and 1960s swung over to the opposite extreme of pellet-only diets in the 1980s and has swung back to a middle ground of a varied diet that includes many different kinds of foods. This type of varied diet is probably closest to how wild parrots feed in their native lands, and it offers your bird an opportunity to eat different foods that are healthy and interesting.

To give your lovebird a varied diet, provide him with a bowl of pellets in his cage at all times. Supplement the pellets with another bowl (or water bottle) of fresh, clean water (remember to change this at least once a day to ensure that he drinks only clean water), and give him an additional bowl of fresh foods, such as fruits, vegetables, and seeds. Change the fresh food bowl frequently (after about two hours under normal indoor temperatures) to protect your lovebird from eating possibly spoiled food and becoming ill.

Making Seeds Part of the Diet

Most people think that pet birds should eat birdseed, and they're partly right. Although birdseed alone is not an adequate diet for lovebirds (or any other pet parrot), it can and should be part of the food you feed your pet each day. Many lovebird species have been seen eating different types of seeds in the wild, which means that they are probably a familiar food to your pet bird too.

Seeds are not considered a complete bird diet because they lack some important vitamins and minerals that your bird needs to maintain his

Seeds are a perfectly fine choice to anchor your lovebird's diet, but they do not constitute a complete diet.

health. But seeds have a place in your lovebird's diet because they do provide important fats and are a good energy source.

When you choose seeds for your lovebird, try to purchase them in a store that sells a lot of bird food. Stores with seed packages that sell quickly are likely to provide fresher seeds than those with packages that sit on the shelves for weeks or months.

If you purchase your seeds from bulk bins, select seeds that appear fresh and clean. Don't purchase seeds that have bugs crawling in them or flying near them, and don't purchase any seeds that have webs or excessive dust on them. Don't buy any seeds that smell musty or moldy, and don't buy any that appear wet. Freeze your seeds after you bring them home to kill any insect eggs that may be in them, and store them in your refrigerator to help them stay fresh.

The best way to test the freshness of the seeds you offer your lovebird is to sprout them. To sprout seeds, soak them with water, then drain off the excess. Let the seeds sit on a windowsill in a small dish or in a plastic bag. You should see the seeds begin to sprout in two to three days if they are fresh. Rinse the sprouts and feed them to your lovebird. Store

Feeding Schedule

Your lovebird will need to eat at least twice a day. Provide him with a fresh bowl of pellets and a clean dish of water in the morning, and supplement the pellets with a dish of fresh foods, such as fruits and vegetables. Remove the fresh foods after about two hours to protect your pet from eating spoiled food.

If your schedule offers you time at home during the day, offer your pet an additional tray of fresh foods around lunchtime. Remove them promptly to protect your bird's health.

Offer your bird an additional tray of fresh foods in the late afternoon so that he can enjoy a light dinner before going to bed. Check his pellet bowl at dinnertime and refill it if it's empty, or replace it with a fresh bowl and fresh pellets if he has contaminated it with droppings. Remove the tray of fresh foods at bedtime to ensure that your pet doesn't eat spoiled foods as part of his midnight snack.

Once you set up a feeding schedule for your bird, stick to it as closely as you can. Your bird won't understand that you work Monday through Friday and like to sleep in on the weekends—he will expect breakfast at the same time every morning. Be prepared to get your bird his breakfast and to spend a little time with him on weekends before you crawl back into bed for a little more sleep.

Like seeds, pellets have their advantages as a basis for your lovebird's diet, but they cannot provide everything your bird needs to remain healthy.

the sprouted seeds in the refrigerator for up to three days, then discard any that you haven't fed to your bird. Also, discard any sprouts that smell bad or begin to grow mold because they aren't healthy for your bird.

Up to 25 percent of a pet bird's diet can be seed, but check with your bird's breeder or the staff of the bird store where you purchased him to see what amount of seed he's been accustomed to in his diet.

Providing a Pelleted Diet

As mentioned earlier, pellets became a popular food item for pet birds in the 1980s. Bird food manufacturers created them to provide more balanced nutrition for birds and easier feeding for owners. Pellet diets eliminated the possibility that a bird would pick through his food bowl and eat only

Eating Well

Never ever starve your bird to induce him to switch from a seed diet to a pellet diet. It's cruel, unsafe, and inhumane.

breeding, and maintenance formulas of the same diet in your pet supply store. Young birds need a growth formula to attain their full weight and size; breeding birds need a breeding formula to provide additional nutrition as they lay eggs and raise chicks; and adult pet birds need a maintenance formula to keep them at a healthy weight and on a proper diet. If your lovebird becomes ill, you may encounter another type of formulated diet—a medicated one that your avian veterinarian may prescribe to help your pet regain his health.

Pelleted diets provide a better balance of avian nutrition than a diet comprising a heavily seed-based diet, but a pelleted diet will work only if your bird recognizes the pellets as food

The Organic Option

Some lovebird owners may want to take an organic approach when feeding their birds. Organic produce and even organic bird diets are now widely available, so lovebird owners can give their pets pesticide-free foods. You can find organic produce at many grocery stores and farmers' markets. Many pet supply stores sell organic bird food as well because several major bird food makers have jumped onto the organic bandwagon.

his favorite seeds because pellets combined all the vital nutrients into one food item.

These formulated diets come in two main types: extruded foods, which are pasteurized and formed into shapes at high temperatures, and pellets, which are steam cooked and formed into pellets at slightly lower temperatures.

Formulated diets help to provide optimum nutrition for a bird at different life stages, which is why you're likely to find growth,

Fruits, vegetables, and treats like millet sprays can be added to your bird's diet regularly to ensure health and happiness.

and eats them willingly. If your lovebird is already accustomed to a pelleted diet, he will continue to eat it if it's offered in your home. If he isn't used to a pelleted diet, be patient with him as you transition him onto one.

To do this, offer pellets as part of his normal diet and gradually increase the amount of pellets you provide each day while decreasing the amount of seeds. If your bird doesn't seem interested in the pellets after trying this approach for several days, soak the pellets in fruit juice or pasta sauce to give them a flavor that's familiar to your bird. In time, he will begin to accept pellets as part of his diet. (For more feeding tips, see the "Encouraging a Finicky Eater" sidebar.)

If you're trying to convert your bird to a pelleted diet, make sure that he's eating during the transition period. As mentioned earlier, the best pelleted diet won't work if your bird won't eat, and starving a bird into eating a new food is never recommended.

Pellet Pros and Cons

When pelleted diets first appeared on the market, many bird owners thought that they were the perfect product to feed to a pet bird. Over time, though, it became apparent that there were both positives and negatives to feeding a pelleted diet. The positives included:

- a more balanced approach to avian nutrition
- an easy-to-serve food
- a food that was less likely to spoil in warm weather

Treat Time!

Lovebirds love millet sprays, so offer your bird a special treat by providing him with a millet spray from time to time. Millet sprays for lovebirds are like candy or cookies for people.

Other types of treats are available at your pet supply store. These include sticks and bars that incorporate grains and bits of fruits and vegetables, toys that include cookies and nuts, and fruit-flavored mineral blocks and other chew toys.

Offer treats sparingly as part of your lovebird's diet because he'll overindulge if he's allowed to eat his treats at will. Use treats as part of your training routine (discussed more in Chapter 6), and offer them as occasional rewards for good behavior.

- a food that was easy for birds to eat and digest

Once birds routinely began to eat pelleted diets, bird owners began to discover some negative aspects of feeding pellets. These included:

- a bland taste to the pellets
- an unfamiliar diet in the bird's eyes
- a monotonous diet that lacked the variety of a bird's natural diet in the wild

Although pelleted diets are often marketed as "complete avian nutrition,"

51

You know what they say—the path to a lovebird's heart is through his stomach.

it's best to supplement them with some fruits and vegetables to offer your lovebird a variety of foodstuffs at mealtime. The variety of food choices offers your pet some mental stimulation that a pellet-only diet wouldn't provide, and he needs to feel as if he's foraging a little for his food as he would in the wild.

Read the labels on the different brands of pelleted diets available at your pet supply store, and discuss your bird's nutritional needs with the store staff and with your avian veterinarian if you're unsure of which brand.

As much as your lovebirds love their food and treats, you must always moderate their diet to keep them slim and healthy.

Adding Fruits and Vegetables

Fruits and vegetables are important additions to your lovebird's diet because they provide important vitamins that seeds lack. Vegetables also provide carbohydrates, and fruits offer quick energy in the form of natural sugars.

One of the most important vitamins found in vegetables and fruits is vitamin A, which helps to build up a bird's immune system and protect him from disease. Vitamin A-rich fruits and vegetables include sweet potatoes, broccoli, carrots, papaya, apricots, and cantaloupe.

Some other fruits and vegetables can do double duty for your lovebird because not only do they supply important nutrients, but they also can be a fun and different treat for your bird. These foods include whole green beans, peas in the pod, sections of papaya or pomegranate with exposed seeds, and sliced grape halves. (Grapes can be served with the seeds in place—they are not toxic to birds, and many birds enjoy playing with them.)

Your lovebird's diet can contain up to 50 percent vegetables and about 10 percent fruit. You can feed your lovebird almost any fruit or vegetable to improve his diet, but there are a few to avoid. These include iceberg and other light green lettuces, which have little nutritional value, and avocado and rhubarb, which can be poisonous to pet birds. Also, remove any fruit pits and apple seeds before feeding fruits to your bird because they contain trace amounts of cyanide.

FAMILY-FRIENDLY TIP

How a Child Can Help to Feed the Bird

Children of all ages can help to select fresh vegetables and fruits for the bird at the supermarket. With adult assistance, they also can take part in washing the produce before it is served to the bird.

Children of all ages (with help from their parents) also can help to select the bird's pelleted food, along with his treats, at the pet store. Older children (aged 8 and up) can change food and water dishes in the cage during morning and evening feedings. Teenaged children can help to prepare and serve the bird's fresh foods.

Most lovebirds appreciate being served fresh vegetables and fruits. Wash the produce with some dish soap and water, then rinse thoroughly and dry with paper towels before serving it to your bird. Washing the fruits and vegetables with soap and water will remove dust, dirt, and any bacteria the produce may have been exposed to prior to coming to your home.

For something a little different, occasionally try steaming or microwaving the vegetables. Be sure that the vegetables have cooled adequately before serving them to your lovebird so that they don't burn him.

You're Eating It, I Want It

You may notice that your lovebird takes an interest in whatever you're eating, so be prepared to share. Your bird will probably come to expect his own portion of whatever you're eating because in the wild, flock members eat together, and you are part of your bird's flock in your home.

Foods that are safe to share include pastas, vegetables and fruits, unsweetened cereals, waffles or pancakes without syrup or butter, unbuttered toast, cooked oatmeal, and unsalted crackers, nuts, and pretzels.

You also can offer small portions of well-cooked meat or poultry, scrambled eggs, and dairy products. Keep in mind, though, that your lovebird lacks the ability to digest large amounts of milk products, so limit his access to cheese and milk to keep his digestive system healthy.

You can offer lovebird-sized portions of any healthy people food you're eating, as long as you don't give your pet anything you've just taken a bite of. Human saliva contains bacteria that are perfectly normal for humans but that are potentially very harmful to your lovebird. Sharing is good, but everyone should have his or her own plate at snack time or mealtime. By the same token, don't kiss your bird directly on his beak or let him preen your lips or teeth. This will ensure that he isn't exposed to the bacteria in your mouth.

The Overweight Lovebird

One of the most common problems that avian veterinarians see in their

Watch your lovebird's diet carefully. Even though they are small, lovebirds can become overweight if they take in more calories than they burn while exercising.

practices is the obese, or overweight, parrot. Although lovebirds are not as prone to becoming overweight as some other parrots are, it's still possible that your lovebird could someday have a weight problem. If your lovebird takes in more calories at mealtime than he burns off during the day by exercising, he may become overweight.

Signs of obesity in a pet bird include buildup of fat on the bird's upper chest or belly. An overweight bird also may develop gaps between his feathers where the fat peeks through, or he may sit with a wide-legged stance on his perch. An obese bird can run out of breath quickly, and he may not be as active as he once was.

You can help your lovebird stay trim by ensuring that he has plenty of opportunities for exercise during the day. Give him ladders to climb and toys to play with and maybe even a swing to swing on in his cage, and provide him with plenty of fresh fruits and vegetables at mealtime. Limit his access to high-fat seed mixes and treats, and you should soon have your bird looking good!

Chapter 4

Looking Good

Grooming is an important part of your responsibilities as a lovebird owner because it's an important part of your pet's normal care routine. Regular grooming not only helps keep a lovebird looking good, but the routine keeps him feeling good. The hands-on routine of grooming also gives you a chance to detect subtle changes in your pet's appearance that may signal a health problem.

Notify your veterinarian if your lovebird's feathers start falling out in patches or if his nails or beak become brittle and overgrown quickly. All of these signs indicate potential health problems that should not be ignored.

Lovebirds spend part of their days grooming themselves, but they can use a little help from their owners to ensure that their feathers are in tip-top shape. Grooming time can be social time for you and your pet too, so make the most of it, especially if you have a single pet lovebird. Lovebirds and other parrots are naturally social creatures that spend time grooming fellow flock members, so your bird will require

Grooming as Quality Time

Although many birds initially don't enjoy the grooming process, the time you spend with your pet as you check and trim his feathers and nails can turn into quality bonding time.

Remember to be patient with your pet and to handle him calmly. Talk to him as you check his nails and feathers, and praise him for being a good bird during the process. Spend some time petting him and scratching some of his favorite tickle spots at the conclusion of your grooming session so that it ends on a positive note for him. In time, he will likely be more tolerant of grooming, and he may even come to enjoy having his feathers and nails trimmed.

Preening is natural for a lovebird, but if you bathe him using some type of conditioner, he may start to preen too much in order to remove the residue from his wings.

regular interaction with you, not only to keep him looking good but feeling like his social needs are being met.

Preening

This is the part of grooming your lovebird can handle himself. A healthy lovebird will spend quite a bit of time each day fluffing and straightening his feathers. He will preen each one that he can reach with his beak. Your bird will probably do most of his preening after he's taken a bath, although birds also preen their dry feathers to help to keep them in condition.

Bathing

As mentioned in Chapter 1, most lovebirds bathe eagerly each day, so be sure to give your pet an opportunity to take a bath. You can do this by providing a shallow dish of lukewarm water in his cage, by misting him with clean water, or by allowing him to stand under a gentle spray of water in the kitchen or bathroom sink. (Be sure that you haven't recently cleaned the sink with chemicals, or your pet could be overcome by harmful fumes.)

If your bird is reluctant to bathe, you may have to employ a simple trick to tempt him into trying a bath. Offer him some damp romaine lettuce or other leafy greens because he will likely roll around on the leaves as he eats and plays with them. Some birds

The Expert Knows

Beware of Conditioning Products

When you walk down the bird care aisle of your pet supply store, you may see different products that are marketed at conditioning your bird's feathers. These shampoos and conditioners are not good for your bird; in fact, they may cause him to begin picking his feathers. Birds preen their feathers every day to remove dirt and other foreign materials, so a bird who has conditioning products on his feathers will preen them until the product is gone. Such enthusiastic preening can become a habit, and this habit can be very difficult to break. For your lovebird's health and well-being, use only clean, warm water on his feathers. This will encourage him to preen normally without creating a potential bad habit.

prefer bathing in this manner, while others will transition to a bathtub or mister bottle after they find out how much fun bath time can be.

Offer your lovebird an opportunity to bathe early in the day so that he has time to preen and dry his feathers before bedtime. You may find that your bird enjoys a little time in the sun after his bath to sit and preen himself. (Make sure that he isn't in direct sun so that he doesn't overheat.) If it's a cool day, help your bird's feathers dry by blowing him with a blow dryer set on the lowest setting. Keep the

Before trimming your lovebird's nails, wrap him comfortably in a towel to keep him feeling safe and secure, and to prevent him from fussing too much.

Lovebird Grooming Supplies

- an assistant to hold your bird while you trim his wings/nails
- an old towel in which to wrap your pet during nail and wing trimming
- nail clippers of the appropriate size for lovebirds (these can either be new human nail clippers or pet nail clippers designed for small parrots)
- styptic powder to stop bleeding on nails
- nail file to smooth rough edges
- small, sharp scissors for wing trimming
- needle-nose pliers to remove damaged blood feathers
- cornstarch to stop bleeding during wing trimming

dryer moving so that your bird doesn't overheat while his feathers are drying.

Nail Care

Your lovebird has four toes on each foot, and each toe has a nail. These nails need to be monitored regularly to ensure that they don't become overgrown. They must be trimmed to keep them in good condition.

If your lovebird has light-colored nails, trimming them will be a bit easier than if he has darker nails. Light-colored nails give you a chance to see where the nail ends and where the quick (the nerve and blood supply for the nail) begins. If your bird has darker nails, you may choose to have your veterinarian's office handle the nail-trimming duties to ensure that your pet's nails aren't trimmed too deeply.

The goal of trimming your bird's nails is to remove just the hooked portion of the nail. This protects your pet from injury because he won't be able to catch his nails on his cage or toys. Trim your bird's nails carefully, and remove small portions of the nail as you trim to ensure that you don't cut too deeply.

To cut your bird's nails, you'll first need to catch him in a towel. To do this, drape the towel over your hand diagonally so that you have one corner above your hand and the rest of the towel below your hand. (This larger portion will be wrapped around your bird's body.) Gently take hold of your bird behind his head and lift him out of his cage, wrapping his body in the towel as you take him out. Don't constrict his chest area too tightly because he needs to be able to breathe freely.

Lay your bird on his back and take one foot out of the towel. Allow him to chew on the towel while you cut and file each nail individually. Praise him for being a good bird, and spend some time cuddling him after you've finished trimming his nails so that he will think that grooming time is a pleasant experience in the future.

Beak Care

Under normal circumstances, you will not need to have your bird's beak trimmed. Birds do a good job of keeping their beaks in condition if they receive a variety of chew toys and live in a healthy environment.

61

Keeping your lovebird's nails trimmed is an important part of keeping your bird safe, but it can be harrowing for new bird owners. Consult your vet if you're too nervous to try it yourself.

Grooming for Good Health

The time you spend grooming your bird is an important investment in his overall good health. Birds are highly skilled at hiding signs of illness, so by the time you notice something unusual in your bird's appearance or habits, he may be quite ill.

As you check the length of his feathers, take time to look for signs of injury, such as lumps, bumps, or swelling. Also, determine whether your bird has any unexplained bald patches or if he's recently begun pulling out some of his feathers. Note the condition of his feathers, too: Are there any holes or discolored areas on the feathers? Stress bars, which often show up as white lines across the width of a feather, may indicate an underlying illness, so report any feather changes to your veterinarian's office.

As you groom your bird's nails, check his feet for signs of tenderness or inflammation. If you find anything out of the ordinary, contact your veterinarian's office for an appointment so that you can help your bird get healthy as quickly as possible.

If you notice that your lovebird's beak seems overgrown, contact your veterinarian's office for an appointment. An overgrown beak may indicate an underlying health problem. If a health problem is the cause, it should be treated promptly to help your bird have the best chance of recovery. Don't try to trim your bird's beak yourself because it contains a large number of blood vessels. Trimming it at home could harm your bird, which is why it's better to let your veterinarian handle this chore.

Wing Trimming

Before we look at the fundamentals of wing trimming, let's first discuss why a bird's wings should be trimmed. A bird should have his wings trimmed to keep him from flying away unexpectedly. Birds with untrimmed wings are likely to fly out an open window or door, even if they've never shown an interest in flying. If a bird with untrimmed wings is startled or spooked and an open window is nearby, chances are he will be out the window before you know what has happened. In addition, birds with untrimmed wings are less likely to be recovered by their owners. Trimmed wings also help to keep your pet safe while he's in your home because he can't fly unexpectedly into the ceiling fan or splash down into the toilet or fish tank.

For your bird's safety, both his wings should be trimmed. Some experts recommend trimming only one wing, but that isn't very safe because it causes a bird to fly unevenly. The goal of trimming a bird's wings is to give him enough flight feathers to glide to a controlled stop if he flies off the top of his cage and lands on the ground, but not enough flight-feather length to allow him to fly free.

You'll probably find that your lovebird is easier to handle after his wings are trimmed. Some birds get a bit saucy when their wing feathers grow in, and trimming the feathers helps rein in some of their more mischievous attitude.

If you're not sure about trimming your bird's wings yourself, ask your avian veterinarian to demonstrate the process for you. After watching how it's done, you may feel confident enough to try it on your own. The following instructions will walk you through the process step by step.

Trimming your bird's wings, while also important, is another health care measure nervous new owners might want to leave to their veterinarians.

Step One

First, gather all your grooming supplies. (See the "Lovebird Grooming Supplies" sidebar for details on the tools you will need.) Then find a well-lit place in your home that's quieter than the rest of your house and set up your supplies. Some birds find grooming to be a stressful procedure, so it's best for both of you if you can start with a quiet location.

Ask someone else in the house to help you hold your bird while you trim his wings. Having someone else hold him means that you can concentrate on trimming, which will make the process go more smoothly.

Step Two

After you've set up your supplies, catch your lovebird in a towel (see the "Nail Care" section for information on how to do this) and have your assistant lay him on his back. Have your assistant hold his head securely so that he doesn't wiggle too much. Make sure that he can breathe easily, and talk quietly to him to keep him calm during the trimming process.

Gently pull one wing away from

Stopping the Blood Flow

Before you groom your bird, you should be familiar with how to stop him from bleeding in the event that a blood feather or toenail is cut too deeply. Birds don't have a large volume of blood in their bodies, so it's important to know how to control bleeding.

In the event that a blood feather is cut, that feather must be removed. To do this, use needle-nose pliers to grasp the feather shaft as close to your bird's skin as you can and pull it out of his body. Remove the feather shaft with one smooth motion, and pinch the skin closed after the feather shaft has been removed. Hold it for several minutes to stop the blood flow. If your bird continues to bleed, put a pinch of flour or cornstarch on the site of the bleeding and continue to apply direct pressure. If the bleeding does not stop, contact your veterinarian's office for assistance.

While it may seem as though removing the blood feather is hurting your lovebird, think about it in this way: The broken feather shaft provides an opening for blood to flow out of your bird's body, so removing the shaft is the best way to control the bleeding.

If you cut your bird's toenail too deeply, apply a pinch of cornstarch or flour, followed by direct pressure, to stop the bleeding. If he does not stop bleeding, contact your veterinarian's office for immediate assistance.

your bird's body and examine it for blood feathers. These feathers, which are still growing in, will be darker and waxier than the other feathers in your bird's wing. Do not cut the blood feathers. If your bird has a lot of them, delay the wing-trimming

Be as gentle as possible when trimming your bird's wings, and always remember to give him words of praise and encouragement for being a good bird.

process for a few days to allow them a chance to develop. If your bird only has one or two, it's safe to trim the rest of his wing feathers—just remember to trim the blood feathers after they've finished growing in.

Step Three
To trim your bird's feathers, separate each one from other flight feathers in the wing and cut it individually. Hold your bird's wing with one hand and cut with the other to ensure that the wing stays steady as you're cutting. Don't cut several feathers at once because your bird could pull his wing out of position, which could cause you to cut more than his feathers.

Start from the tip of the wing when you trim, and clip the first five feathers in. (You may have to trim a few more feathers if your lovebird can still fly well after his first five flight feathers are trimmed.) Use the set of feathers above the primary flight feathers— they're called the coverts—as your

guide for final feather length, and trim the flight feathers so that they are a little longer than the coverts.

Trim each wing separately, and clip each one carefully. Trim the same number of feathers on each wing. This will help your bird maintain his balance when gliding.

Step Four

Once you finish the initial trim, have your assistant let your bird out of the towel. Cuddle him and praise him for being good during the trimming, then let him play on his playgym or in his cage. If you notice that he's still able to fly well, catch him in the towel again and trim off two or three more flight feathers on each wing.

Keep an eye on the length of your lovebird's feathers, and plan to trim them after his molt, as well as whenever you notice they're growing long enough for him to fly well. Most bird owners trim their birds' wings about four times a year.

The Annual Molt

At least once a year, your lovebird will lose his feathers. He will molt his old feathers in a symmetrical pattern, and

66

Molting can be an uncomfortable time for new bird owners, but don't worry—in a short time, your bird will look as beautiful and vibrant as ever.

How Your Children Can Help to Groom Your Bird

Before you involve your children in grooming your lovebird, you'll need to consider their ages and their personalities. Young or excitable children can help you gather the grooming supplies before your bird comes out of his cage, but it's probably best for both them and your bird if they are elsewhere when the actual grooming takes place.

Preteen or teenaged children can help you groom your bird by acting as your grooming assistant, provided they are calm around the bird and will take direction from you without getting excited.

The goal is to make grooming your bird a quick and reasonably stress-free activity, so use your best judgment as to how involved your children should be.

keratin sheaths. These new feathers look like they are wrapped in plastic, or they may resemble the ends of a shoelace. As the feathers finish developing, the sheath starts to break down, and your bird will begin preening it off to expose his new feathers.

Be watchful of your bird's wing feathers at molting time. As soon as his new wing feathers have grown in, trim his flight feathers so that he cannot fly away from you in case a window or door is accidentally left open.

You may notice that your bird seems a bit out of sorts as he's molting, or he may decide to be extra friendly to you because you can help him preen some of the feathers that are difficult for him to reach. Preen such feathers gently because they may be a bit more sensitive to your touch than your bird's older feathers.

67

he won't lose too many feathers all at once. By losing just a few feathers at a time from each side of his body, your bird maintains his ability to flee from predators just as he would in the wild.

As your bird loses his old feathers, his new ones come in covered in

Chapter 5

Feeling Good

Lovebirds are remarkably sturdy little animals, but they can become ill from time to time, and when they do, it's often a serious situation. Preventing illness in your pet is much easier than treating it after the fact, so it's important to locate a veterinarian with expertise in treating pet birds who can help to keep your lovebird healthy.

To help your lovebird maintain his health and live a long life, he should visit the veterinarian soon after you bring him home and then at least once a year thereafter. If he's sick, he'll have to go more often in order to receive treatment.

Your lovebird also may visit the veterinarian's office more frequently if the clinic offers grooming services because you may feel more comfortable having a staff member trim his wings and nails. In addition, you may want to take advantage of the clinic's boarding facilities when you go out of town. Having the clinic staff groom and board your bird gives them additional opportunities to see him, which can help them detect and treat potential health problems before they become serious.

Bird Health Insurance

Many avian veterinarians accept health insurance for pet birds. Pet bird health insurance, which has been available since the late 1990s, helps to cover the cost of surgical procedures, prescriptions, diagnostic tests, and routine care. Ask your veterinarian's office for more information on pet health insurance.

As a caring lovebird owner, you play an important role in your pet's health care team. It's up to you to learn what's normal for your pet's daily routine and his food and water consumption, and to take him to the veterinarian if you notice anything out of the ordinary in his routine or appearance. Feed him the healthiest food you possibly can, and provide him with plenty of fresh, clean water each day. Also, make sure that his cage tray is cleaned daily and that the cage is scrubbed and disinfected each

Find an avian practice specialist if you can, but no matter what, you must choose a veterinarian. with ample experience with pet birds.

week. Finally, his surroundings must be safe to ensure that he doesn't fall ill or become injured.

How to Select a Veterinarian

Ideally, you will want to choose a veterinarian for your bird who is an avian practice specialist. Avian practice specialists are veterinarians with a particular interest in birds who have taken special examinations from the American Board of Veterinary Practitioners (ABVP). If you cannot find an avian practice specialist in your area, try to locate a veterinarian who is a member of the Association of Avian Veterinarians (AAV) or who at least has a long-standing interest in pet birds.

Ask the breeder or bird specialty store staff where you purchased your lovebird for veterinary recommendations. If you have bird-owning friends, they may be able to recommend a veterinarian, or you can call bird clubs in your area for referrals.

If you are unable to locate a veterinarian by referral, your next best bet is to search the phone book or Internet. Look for yellow page ads that list bird care as a clinic specialty, or do an online search for "bird vet [your city and state]."

After you've found a couple of bird-friendly veterinary clinics, call them and ask a few questions, such as how many birds the practice sees in a month, if any of the veterinarians or other staff members keep birds themselves, what a routine office visit might cost, and what forms of payment are accepted.

Finding an Emergency Clinic

Try to locate an animal emergency clinic at the same time you choose your bird's regular veterinarian. With luck, your bird's regular clinic will offer after-hours care, but if that's not possible, ask for referrals to emergency clinics in your area. Write down directions to the clinic from your home, as well as the clinic's address and phone number, before an emergency occurs. Put this information in an easy-to-find place, such as the glove compartment of your car or on top of your bird's travel carrier so that you will have it in the event of an emergency.

When you find an office that sounds like it's a good fit for your bird, set up an appointment for him to be evaluated. Write down any questions that you have about your lovebird's care before the appointment so that you can ask the doctor or office staff about them. Plan to arrive at least 15 minutes ahead of your scheduled appointment time for the first office visit so that you can fill out any new patient paperwork the office requires.

Visiting the Veterinarian

Your lovebird's first visit to the veterinarian's office will probably be for a routine examination. If you have other birds in your home, schedule

Feeling Good

this examination on your way home from the breeder or bird specialty store. If this is not possible, have your bird examined as soon as possible after he comes into your home, and keep him in quarantine for about 60 days to ensure that he doesn't pass any illnesses to the other birds in your home. If your lovebird will be a single pet bird, the quarantine process is not necessary.

At your first office visit, your lovebird will probably be evaluated first by a veterinary technician, who will weigh him and will ask you some basic questions about the reason for the bird's visit to the clinic, as well as his daily routine and diet. The technician functions much as a nurse or clinical assistant does at your doctor's office, taking the patient's vital signs and making some notes on his chart.

After the technician finishes with your bird, the veterinarian will come into the exam room. She will first look at your lovebird in his travel carrier. This gives your bird a few minutes to adjust to the veterinarian before the actual examination begins. The veterinarian may ask you additional questions about your bird or ask if you have any questions before starting to examine him.

Keeping your lovebird hale and hearty is one of your greatest responsibilities as a bird owner.

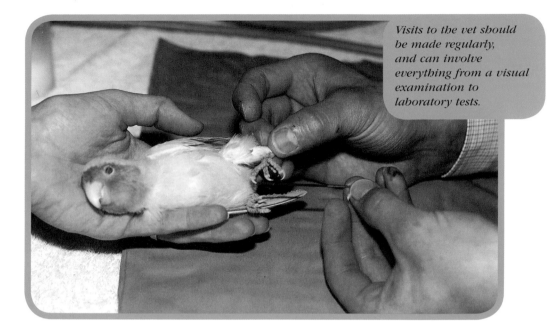

During the actual examination, the veterinarian will pay special attention to your lovebird's eyes, beak, and nares (nostrils). She will examine your bird's mouth for signs of infection. She also will check your bird's wings and body for abnormalities by carefully touching and feeling his body. In addition, the vet will check the condition of your lovebird's feathers, legs, feet, and vent (the opening through which the bird eliminates waste and lays eggs).

Lab Tests

After the physical examination concludes, the veterinarian may recommend some laboratory tests be done on your lovebird, including blood work, X-rays, and fecal screens. Each has its own part in helping to maintain your bird's health. Here is a little more detail on each type of test:

- **Blood work:** Blood work, which includes a complete blood count or a blood chemistry profile, helps the veterinarian determine whether or not your lovebird has a specific illness.

- **X-rays:** X-rays allow the veterinarian to see inside your lovebird's body to determine whether he has any broken bones or whether he has ingested a foreign object. They also give the veterinarian a view of his internal organs.

- **Fecal screens:** Fecal screens help the veterinarian determine whether a lovebird has internal parasites or infections.

At the conclusion of the exam, the veterinarian will ask if you have

FAMILY-FRIENDLY TIP

Explaining the Vet Visit to Your Child

To help your child understand what happens at the vet's office, you'll need to explain what will likely go on during the pet's examination. Explain that the doctor and possibly technicians and nurses will weigh your pet, handle him carefully, and give him a physical that may include looking at the condition of his feet and feathers, listening to his heart, checking his eyes and nares (nostrils), and examining the inside of his mouth. The doctor and staff will probably ask questions about your lovebird's diet and his normal daily activities as well and may then recommend some tests and set up a routine examination schedule for your pet.

any questions, so discuss any that you have with her or a member of the clinic staff. Make sure that you understand the answers completely, and ask if it's okay to call the clinic if you think of

additional questions later. Schedule any follow-up appointments as you leave the clinic.

Under normal circumstances, your lovebird will need to visit the veterinarian for an annual checkup. Birds with underlying illnesses or other medical conditions will need to visit the veterinarian more frequently for follow-up treatments that will help them regain their health.

Signs of Illness

Detecting signs of illness in your lovebird is an important part of bird ownership. Lovebirds and other parrots are very, very good at disguising the fact that they are sick, so it's up to you to learn what's normal for your bird and what behaviors aren't quite right.

Please note that veterinarians talk about *signs* of illness, rather than

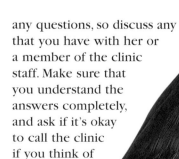

Signs that Your Lovebird Needs Immediate Care

Contact your avian veterinarian's office immediately if you see your bird showing any of these signs:

- The bird is bleeding.
- The bird has a damaged or missing upper beak.
- The bird has recently flown into a window or mirror.
- The bird was exposed to toxic fumes or has eaten something poisonous.
- The bird was bitten or clawed by another pet in the home.
- The bird cannot breathe properly.
- The bird is straining to eliminate, but no droppings are coming out.

symptoms. Symptoms tend to indicate that a patient can tell his doctor what the problem is. While many parrots are talkative, they aren't chatty enough to be able to tell the veterinarian where it hurts, so the doctor has to rely on outward signs of illness.

By the time a lovebird is showing signs of illness, he is probably quite ill, so it's important to alert your veterinarian's office to changes in your bird's normal routine immediately.

Here are some signs of illness to watch out for:

- The bird is fluffed up all the time.
- The bird has no appetite.
- The bird sleeps a lot more than he normally does.

Abnormal behavior from your bird can be an indication that your bird is not totally healthy.

- The bird eliminates more or less often than normal.
- The bird's droppings look very different than normal.
- The bird has lost weight.
- The bird has no interest in his surroundings or toys.
- The bird's wings are droopy.
- The bird has become lame.
- The bird has food stuck to his facial feathers.
- The bird has regurgitated onto the cage floor.
- The bird's tail bobs when he breathes.
- The bird cannot breathe easily.
- The bird has discharge coming from his eyes or nares.
- The bird has stopped talking or singing.

Feeling Good

If you suspect that your lovebird might be ill, the best policy is always to take your bird to the veterinarian. You're better off safe than sorry.

An Avian First-Aid Kit

Here are some supplies you should have on hand in case you need to provide first aid to your lovebird:

- a heat source, such as a heating pad
- bandages
- cornstarch or styptic powder to control bleeding
- disinfectant solution
- energy supplement, such as Gatorade
- eye dropper
- grooming tools (nail clippers, nail file, needle-nose pliers)
- saline solution
- scissors with rounded tips
- small flashlight
- small towels for catching and holding your bird
- tweezers

Pet Bird Illnesses

Although they are normally hardy little parrots, lovebirds can contract a number of different diseases. Some common ones are outlined in this section. All require veterinary care to be treated effectively.

If your bird shows signs of illness, don't try to treat him with over-the-counter medications sold at your pet store before taking him to the veterinarian. Although you may see this as a money- and time-saving approach, it isn't. Your veterinarian needs to determine what is making your bird sick so that he can receive specific medications targeted to kill the organisms that are causing the illness. Over-the-counter medications are too broad spectrum to work effectively, and administering them wastes precious time that your bird could be using to recover with the correct medications.

Now let's look at some of the most

common diseases that lovebirds can contract. (These diseases are listed in alphabetical order for easy reference.)

Aspergillosis

Aspergillosis is named for the fungus, *Aspergillis*, that causes it. This disease causes breathing difficulties in affected birds because it settles in their respiratory system. Birds with pre-existing health conditions or birds who have recently been ill are more at risk for catching aspergillosis than are healthy birds.

Your veterinarian can prescribe antifungal drugs to treat this disease, which can be prevented easily by keeping your bird's cage and surrounding environment clean and by using only newspaper, paper towels, or used computer paper (rather than ground corncobs or walnut shells, which encourage fungal growth) to line your bird's cage tray.

Candida

This disease is also named for the organism that causes it—a yeast called *Candida albicans*. Young birds or birds who have recently recovered from another illness are more likely to catch candida than are healthy adult birds. A bird with candida will have cheesy white growths in his mouth, and he will have lost his appetite. He also will regurgitate frequently and have a slow-emptying crop.

If your bird contracts candida, he needs antifungal drugs prescribed by your veterinarian. Feeding a varied, vitamin A-rich diet is a good way to prevent your lovebird from contracting this disease.

Egg Binding

When a female bird is unable to lay an egg, she is said to be egg bound. She will try to lay the egg, but it is stuck inside her and may need to be removed by a veterinarian. Several factors can cause egg binding, such as an improperly shaped egg, an overbred female bird, or a bird with low blood calcium levels.

If your bird is sitting on the cage floor and is panting a lot or seems to be paralyzed, suspect egg binding. If possible, gently pick the bird up and examine her vent. You may be able to see a partially laid egg sticking out.

Just as with humans, getting your bird treatment for certain illnesses can be unpleasant but necessary.

Run a hot shower and place the egg-bound bird in the warm, humid bathroom. The heat and humidity from the shower may help her pass the egg. Call your veterinarian's office for additional instructions on how to help your egg-bound bird.

Giardia

Like the first two diseases in this section, *Giardia* is also named for the organism that causes it—

Feed your bird a balanced, controlled diet and obesity should never be a problem.

The Dangers of Nonstick Cookware

Nonstick cookware has made cooking easier and quicker, but it's resulted in some unplanned complications for bird owners. Nonstick cookware and some drip pans on household stoves are coated with a chemical called PTFE that makes food less likely to stick to them. If this chemical is heated to 536°F (280°C), it begins to break down and emit a toxic gas that can be deadly to birds.

If you're shopping for new pots and pans, purchase stainless steel cookware and spray it with a nonstick cooking spray. Your pans will be just as clean at the end of the day and your lovebird will be much safer.

Also, take care when using the self-cleaning cycle on your oven. The self-cleaning cycle sometimes can create harmful fumes for pet birds. Use this cycle only after you've opened the windows around your bird's cage to let in fresh air. Before opening the windows, be sure that your lovebird's cage is securely closed to prevent him from escaping through an open window.

a protozoan called *Giardia psittaci*. Although *Giardia* can be difficult for your veterinarian to detect, have

PDDS is a fatal, incurable illness in pet birds. If your pet shows any signs of the syndrome—depression, vomiting, or seizures—consult a veterinarian immediately.

your lovebird tested if he begins to lose weight, pass loose droppings, or pick his feathers. Appetite loss and depression also can indicate a *Giardia* infestation.

Once *Giardia* has been detected in your bird's droppings, your veterinarian can prescribe medications to treat it.

Obesity

While some might not consider it a disease, obesity is at least a condition that sets a pet bird up for potential health problems in the future. In rare cases, obesity in a pet bird can be caused by a thyroid problem, but most pet birds become fat because they consume more calories at mealtime than they burn off through exercise.

As with people, obesity in pet birds can lead to long-term health problems. Overweight birds may develop problems with their bones and joints, and they may become prone to diabetes; thyroid, pancreatic, or liver problems; or heart disease.

Feeding a balanced diet that contains low amounts of walnuts, peanuts, sunflower seeds, and millet is your best defense against creating an overweight bird. Also, make sure that your lovebird has plenty of chances to exercise outside his cage each day, along with a variety of interesting toys that will encourage him to exercise inside his cage.

Polyomavirus

This viral disease, which was originally called French moult, causes problems

Eating a primarily seed-based diet can sometimes increase your lovebird's chances of contracting an upper respiratory infection.

lovebird against polyomavirus. This vaccine is one of the few preventive treatments available to pet bird owners, so ask your veterinarian for more information about it.

Proventricular Dilatation Disease Syndrome (PDDS)

PDDS, formerly known as macaw wasting disease, is a very serious disease of a bird's digestive system that was first discovered in macaws. It was originally thought to be a disease that only affected macaws, but it affects many other species of pet birds.

Birds who have PDDS cannot digest their food properly. They may pass whole seeds or other food items in their droppings. Birds with PDDS also may be depressed, regurgitate frequently, and have seizures. This disease is fatal, and no cure exists at present, although research is underway at the University of Georgia to find a cure.

Psittacine Circovirus 1

This viral disease, originally called psittacine beak and feather disease syndrome, or PBFDS, was originally considered a cockatoo-specific problem. More than 40 parrot species are at risk from this disease, which often shows itself through pinched or

with a bird's flight and tail feathers. Some birds with polyomavirus do not develop flight and tail feathers, while other affected birds have improperly formed feathers.

Birds can catch this disease by coming into contact with sick birds or with dust from the feathers or droppings of a sick bird. Some adult birds are carriers of this disease, which means that they are infected with it but don't show any signs of being sick. These carrier birds can pass polyomavirus to others.

Signs of polyomavirus infection include weakness, appetite loss, diarrhea, paralysis, regurgitation, and bleeding beneath the skin. Your veterinarian can vaccinate your clubbed feathers. Affected birds also can have beak fractures and mouth ulcers. This highly contagious, fatal disease is most common in birds less than three years of age, and there is no cure.

Psittacosis

This disease, which is also called chlamydiosis or parrot fever, may be carried by some birds for their entire lives. The bird may never show clinical signs of illness, but he could pass the disease along.

Birds with psittacosis may pass lime-green droppings, lose their appetites, lose weight, and act depressed. Your avian veterinarian can prescribe a pelleted diet treated with tetracycline, which your bird will have to eat for a certain number of days to be cured.

Psittacosis is a zoonotic disease, or one that can be passed between parrots and people. If someone in your home has recently undergone chemotherapy or is immune suppressed, they may be at risk for catching psittacosis. Under normal conditions, however, catching psittacosis from a pet bird is fairly rare. A person with psittacosis will have flu-like symptoms, so consult your physician if you develop these symptoms after bringing a pet bird into your home. Antibiotic treatment will help to clear up this disease.

Vitamin A Deficiency

Pet birds need vitamin A to keep their immune systems healthy, but some birds, especially those who eat primarily seed-based diets, do not receive enough vitamin A to maintain good health.

Indications that a pet bird is not receiving enough dietary vitamin A include breathing problems, frequent infections, mouth sores, and vision difficulties. This condition can be prevented by providing your bird with a diet rich in vitamin A including such foods as broccoli, sweet potatoes, carrots, dried or fresh red peppers, cantaloupe, papaya, and apricots.

81

Psittacosis can cause your lovebird to pass lime-green droppings, lose his appetite, lose weight, and act depressed, but luckily it can be treated with a special pelleted diet.

Upper Respiratory Infections

Birds who eat primarily seed-based diets may be prone to upper respiratory infections. A bird with an upper respiratory infection may have discharge coming from his nares or eyes, he may bob his tail as he breathes, and he may keep his feathers fluffed at all times.

Your veterinarian can prescribe antibiotics to treat this condition, which can be prevented by feeding a varied diet containing plenty of fresh foods, especially those high in vitamin A.

What to Do if Your Birds Accidentally Mate

If you keep a pair of lovebirds in the same cage, they may at some point go to nest and lay eggs. This may or may not mean that you have a true pair (a male and a female) because some female birds will lay eggs whether a male bird is present or not.

If your lovebirds have between five and seven eggs, chances are they are a true pair. If you see quite a few more eggs, you probably have two female birds who are trying to go to nest at the same time.

Fertile lovebird eggs will hatch in about 23 days, while infertile or clear eggs will never hatch. You can allow your birds to incubate their eggs for about 23 days; then, discard them if none has hatched because they are probably infertile.

If your lovebirds seem determined to lay eggs, set them up with a nest box until they have reared their first clutch of chicks, then remove the nest box to discourage them from further breeding.

Provide additional servings of both pellets and fresh foods, and increase the amount of calcium you are providing to ensure that your female lovebird's health is not endangered by the egg-laying process. If a female bird does not receive enough calcium in her diet while she is laying eggs, her body will draw the calcium it needs to make eggshells out of her bones, which leaves them brittle and more prone to breakage.

Quarantining a sick bird is important if you have multiple birds in your home. You naturally want to keep the sick bird from infecting the healthy ones.

The Importance of Quarantine

Quarantine is a process bird owners use to protect the health of the existing birds in the home against diseases that might be brought in by new birds. Keep your lovebird separate from other birds in your home for at least 60 days to ensure that he hasn't brought in any illnesses. This means keeping him in a different room than your other birds, and it also means that your lovebird gets fed and watered and has his cage cleaned each day after all your other birds have been cared for. Wash your hands thoroughly after you've taken care of your lovebird and before you handle your other birds to protect their health.

After your lovebird has become an established member of your flock, take similar precautions to safeguard his health if you add another bird to your home. Also, if you visit bird stores, bird marts, or even a zoo with a large bird collection, shower and change clothes before you handle your birds to protect them from diseases that you inadvertently may have brought home.

Stress and Your Lovebird's Health

Although stress is part of everyday life for both people and parrots, too much stress can harm your lovebird's health. If you notice your bird has started shaking, screaming, pulling his feathers, or sleeping poorly, he could be feeling overly stressed, which could eventually cause him to become ill. Other signs of stress include your bird sitting up as tall as he can on his perch to appear thin, a loss of appetite, and diarrhea.

To help reduce the stress in your lovebird's life, give him a predictable routine. Serve him his meals at about the same time each day, and provide him with several opportunities each day to exercise and play outside his

When It's an Emergency

In certain situations, your lovebird will need urgent care from you. Following are some emergency situations, along with at-home treatments to try before contacting your veterinarian's office.

Please note that at-home treatment is not a substitute for veterinary care; it is merely an attempt to make your bird comfortable before he is treated by your veterinarian.

Bleeding: Stop bleeding with direct pressure or a pinch of cornstarch. If the bird has a broken blood feather, remove it with needle-nose pliers, then apply cornstarch and direct pressure.

Breathing problems: Place the bird in a steamy, warm room, such as the bathroom with the shower running.

Broken bones: Keep the bird warm and quiet.

Burns: Mist affected area with cool water. Do not apply butter or other greasy substances to the burn.

Frostbite: Keep the bird warm and quiet.

Heatstroke: Cool the bird by placing him in front of a fan or allowing him to stand in a bowl of cool water. Allow the bird to drink cool water or provide him with cool water via an eyedropper.

Seizures: Keep the bird warm and quiet. Transfer him to his travel carrier to protect him from harm.

Shock: Keep the bird warm and quiet.

cage. Clean his cage each week, and rotate his toys after it's been cleaned.

The Care of Older Lovebirds

With good care, a lovebird can live 12 years or more. As lovebirds age, they require a little more attention from their owners than they did when they were younger. One important thing to pay attention to as your lovebird ages is his diet. Older birds need a diet that is lower in fat than younger birds do, so you may have to adjust your pet's diet a bit as he ages.

Because older lovebirds may be prone to arthritis and other joint problems, you may want to provide an additional heat source for your older pet. For example, a small heat lamp can provide adequate heat. Set up the lamp so that your lovebird cannot burn himself on it while being able to sit close enough to it to absorb the heat it provides.

Older lovebirds may be at risk for tumors, vision and thyroid problems, and upper respiratory infections. They may take longer to molt than they did when they were younger, or the condition of their feathers may deteriorate.

Pay special attention to your older lovebird's routine to help to detect health problems before they become serious.

Older birds, like people, can develop arthritis and joint problems, so you need to offer them even more loving care than you did when they were younger.

Chapter 6

Being Good

Now that you know the basics of caring for your lovebird, it's time to discuss how you'll tame and train him. Your lovebird is a clever little parrot, so he should quickly learn some basic behaviors, and you may even be able to teach him some simple tricks!

roper handling and careful training can strengthen the bond between you and your pet, and your lovebird will find things more interesting if you take him out of his cage regularly. For his safety, though, he needs to learn a few simple commands so that you can handle him easily when he's away from his cage. The taming and training process can be one of the most enjoyable parts of owning a lovebird, so be sure to make the time fun for both you and your pet!

Training Time Can Be Treat Time

Food treats are one effective way to positively reinforce your lovebird's good behavior. Use his favorite treat to reward him during training sessions when you first begin the training process, then gradually decrease the number of treats given during training. Substitute praise, cuddles, and petting for food rewards to ensure that your pet still receives positive reinforcement for his good behavior.

Bird Body Language

Although your lovebird may not be a big talker, he can tell you a lot of things about how he is feeling by his body language. Here are some signs to look for:

Aggression: beak clicking, wing lifting over the back, tail fanning, wing drumming, and open-mouthed perching.

Defensiveness: beak clicking, foot raising, wiping beak on the perch, and an open-mouthed attack posture.

Excitement: Feather fluffing, eye pinning (pupils expand, contract, and expand again), and high activity levels.

Jealousy: Biting, screaming, and destructive behaviors.

Possessiveness: Hissing and driving people away from a chosen person or thing.

Threats: Foot tapping, biting, and elevated posture.

Why Train a Lovebird?

You may be wondering why it's necessary to train your lovebird. Training your lovebird helps him channel some of his seemingly boundless energy into learning tricks and other positive behaviors instead of using that same energy to misbehave. Training your lovebird helps you set some boundaries for your bird, which also helps him learn good behavior.

Training your lovebird also means that you and your pet get to spend time together, which is one of the main reasons you first brought your bird home. He needs regular attention from you to maintain his mental well-being, so why not give him some attention by training him? Also, trained lovebirds are easier for their owners to handle, and they're more enjoyable pets as a result.

Always speak kindly to your lovebirds and offer encouragement —they'll know if you're not being nice to them!

Being Good

Negative Reinforcement

So which training methods work and which don't? Before we look at the best ways to train your lovebird in this chapter, let's start with what *doesn't* work. These methods of discipline will not work on a parrot, so don't try them:

- yelling at the bird
- hitting the bird
- locking the bird in a dark room
- throwing the bird (or his cage) on the ground
- throwing things at the bird
- spraying the bird with water

With some supervision, your lovebirds and children should get along just fine and become fast friends.

Bird owners probably tried some or all of these methods on wild-caught parrots over the years, only to find that none of them was effective. In addition to being ineffective, they are cruel and downright mean—two more good reasons not to use them on your lovebird.

Positive Reinforcement

Positive reinforcement works very well when training your lovebird. In fact, it's the way lovebirds and other parrots learn best! To ensure that your pet enjoys the training process, give him positive reinforcement along the

How Your Child Can Help to Train Your Bird

Older children and teenagers can help you train your bird because they may be more inclined to spend time with him each day, reviewing his training and even teaching him new things.

When my stepdaughter, Rhonda, was about 9, she began training her parakeet, Andre, to do tricks. She worked with Andre each day when she came home from school, reviewing things she had already taught him and praising him for doing the behaviors well. She also taught him a few words, which he often repeated in his squeaky little parakeet voice.

Through Rhonda's patient training, Andre learned how to drop coins on a table in front of a chosen person, and he learned to look both ways before leaving her room and entering the main hallway between the bedrooms in her mother's home so that he wouldn't get stepped on.

These training sessions worked because Rhonda wanted to spend time with Andre. She saw that he was a clever little bird who seemed to enjoy learning to do new things. We didn't ask her to train her bird; it was something she wanted to do, and she ended up enjoying him more as a result of the work she put into teaching him to talk and to do tricks.

way. Praise him when he behaves the way you want him to, and occasionally offer him a favorite food treat to keep him interested in his lessons. Other methods of positive reinforcement include the scratching of a favorite spot on the bird's body or a few minutes of bird and owner playtime.

Whenever your bird does something you want him to do, praise him for it. Many bird owners (me included) forget to give their pets positive reinforcement when they behave well. Tell your lovebird he's a good bird when he plays quietly by himself. Not only will you reinforce the good behavior, you will also reward it by paying attention to your naturally social little parrot.

Your Lovebird and Other Pets

One of the most important things you can do for your lovebird is to socialize him properly to other members of your home, including other pets and children. Your lovebird needs to feel comfortable with other members of your family, and your entire family needs to know how to handle interactions between the pets in your home.

For the safety of all animals in your home, supervise your pets whenever your lovebird is out of his cage. Alert other family members when he is out of his cage in case other pets are in the

92

Lovebirds

If you're very patient, diligent, and lucky, you might be able to coax a few words or phrases out of your lovebird.

Notice the black on this young lovebird's beak. Young lovebirds are more likely to learn to do tricks than older birds, so start training your pet when he's young.

house, and don't allow your lovebird to run around the floor of your home because another pet might think that he is a toy.

Here are some things to consider about lovebirds mixing with other pets:

- A cat in your home may think that the lovebird is a new toy and may accidentally claw or bite him.

- A large dog may step on your lovebird, or the dog may knock over a cage or playgym as he gallops through the house. If you have a sighthound, such as a Greyhound or Whippet, he may try to hunt your lovebird instinctively.

- A medium to large snake or frog may view your lovebird as a meal, so keep your lovebird away from these herptile pets.

Your Lovebird and Your Children

With proper supervision, your lovebird and your children should be able to get along quite nicely. Lovebirds are small enough parrots that they should not frighten most children, who are sometimes intimidated by the size and noise level of larger parrots, such as macaws and cockatoos.

Help your children make the most of their relationship with your lovebird by offering consistent guidance. Explain to them that the bird sometimes needs to be left alone in his cage and that he may not want to play all the time. Let them know that the bird may need a daily nap to rest just like they do.

A few ground rules may help you manage the relationship between your lovebird and your children. (They also work for the adult members of your family!) These include:

- Don't surprise the bird.
- Don't yell at the bird.
- Don't poke at the bird with your finger or with a stick.
- Keep the bird inside the house.
- Let the bird have some quiet time each day.
- Handle the bird carefully (if the child is old enough to do so).

Talking

Although almost any parrot is able to talk, some species—the African grey, the budgie, the Quaker parakeet, and some Amazons—are better known for their talking ability. Unfortunately, lovebirds are not noted talkers, so don't expect your bird to be a talkative pet. However, some lovebird owners have reported that their birds have learned a few words, so it's possible that your pet could surprise you with a few spoken words.

If you want to try teaching your lovebird to talk, here are the steps you should follow.

Start Young

Begin teaching your bird to talk when he is young. Younger birds are more likely to want to imitate your voice than older birds are.

Always end your training sessions with lots of love and positive reinforcement. The more your lovebird enjoys training, the more he'll be willing to try.

The most basic aspect of any training is to build your bird's trust in you. If he's new, that means first letting him become comfortable with you, your home, and his cage before pushing for more.

hear your kids or your spouse when the washing machine is running, the phone is ringing, the microwave is beeping, and the television is on. Your lovebird won't find it any easier to hear you over a lot of background noise, so set him up to succeed by having a quiet training place.

Keep a Single Pet Bird

Birds kept in pairs or in aviary situations are less likely to learn to speak because they have other birds to communicate with in their own language. Single pet birds, on the other hand, are more likely to bond with their owners and want to learn to talk.

No Mirrored Toys

Mirrored toys may make your bird think that he's not alone in his cage, and he will try to bond with and talk to the bird in the mirror instead of talking to you.

Set up a Quiet Training Area

When teaching your bird to talk, try to do your training in a quieter part of the house. Think how hard it is to

Clicker Training

Clicker training is a method lovebird owners can use to positively reinforce their bird's good behavior. It uses a small metal clicker to reward good behavior with a distinctive clicking sound that many birds find appealing.

To train your bird to respond to a clicker, first use the clicker in conjunction with a food reward for good behavior. Click the clicker as you give the bird his treat so that he learns to recognize the sound as a positive reward. Gradually decrease the treats during training, and continue to provide the reinforcement by using the clicker.

Your bird might not always cooperate during training, but with enough patience, trust, and positive reinforcement, he should begin to behave better.

Choose a Single Phrase

By sticking with a single phrase, your bird has a better chance of learning and repeating it. Maybe you'll teach him to say "Hello!" or to say his name. Later, you can add to his vocabulary, but it's best to start simple.

Speak Clearly

If you mumble, your bird will too, so be sure to enunciate your words clearly so that he will hear the phrase correctly.

Have the Phrase Make Sense

If you want your bird to say "Hello," say that to him each time you enter the room. If the phrase makes sense in context, you and your family are more likely to use it when talking to him, which makes him more likely to pick it up and repeat it.

Schedule Short Training Sessions

Your lovebird has about a ten-minute attention span, so don't try to cram too much into one training session.

End on a Positive Note

Whenever possible, end your training sessions positively. Your lovebird will sense any frustration or anger on your part if a session isn't going well, so stop while things are going well so that both of you will want to continue the training later.

Be Patient

This goes with the idea of the positive ending mentioned earlier, but it really is important to be patient with your pet. Put a smile in your voice and make your training sessions fun. If you are enjoying the session, chances are your lovebird will too.

What to Do if Your Bird Flies Away

It's a bird owner's worst nightmare: Your bird has just flown out an open door or window. What do you do if this happens to you?

If your bird flies away, here are some things you can do to increase your chances of recapturing him:

- Keep the bird in sight as long as possible.
- Play a tape or CD of your bird's voice to attract his attention.
- Put your bird's cage outside where he can easily see it.
- Put lots of treats on the cage floor to tempt him back inside.

If your bird doesn't come home right away, here are some additional steps to take:

- Let veterinary offices and your local animal shelters know that you've lost your lovebird.
- Put up posters around your neighborhood. Include a description of your bird, your phone number, and the offer of a small reward.

To help to keep your bird from flying away in the first place, make sure that his wings are trimmed regularly. Check his cage door and the cage tray each week when you're cleaning the enclosure to ensure that the door closes securely and that the cage tray can't fall out and leave the cage bottom open.

Keep your doors and windows closed when your bird is out of his cage. Check your window and door screens to ensure that they fit snugly in their frames and that they do not have any holes.

Listen to Your Bird

It may seem like a funny thing to say when we're talking about talking, but take time to listen to your pet after he goes to bed at night. Many parrots make quiet noises to themselves as they drift off to sleep, and some talking birds use that quiet time to practice the words and phrases they already know.

You may be wondering whether or not the talking CDs that are sold in pet supply stores and online work well when teaching a bird to talk. Sometimes they do, and sometimes they don't. Remember that lovebirds aren't noted for their talking ability to begin with, so it's probably better for you to spend one-on-one time with your bird to teach him to talk instead of relying on a prerecorded CD to do it for you.

Training Basics

The first step to successfully training your lovebird to do anything is to gain his trust. Without trust, training is useless and frustrating, so take the time to gain it before you begin training him.

To gain your bird's trust, allow him time to become comfortable in your home. Most lovebirds need about a week to settle into the routine, so wait at least that long to schedule your first training session.

Begin to build trust by talking softly to your bird. Use his name often so that he will get used to the sound of your voice. Sit quietly by his cage several

Try training your bird to do all sorts of fun stuff, from simple acrobatics to more advanced tricks. When it comes to birds, the sky's the limit!

times a day for about 15 minutes at a time during the first few days so that he adjusts to having you nearby. End the session by leaving your bird a treat in his food bowl so that he associates the treat with having you nearby.

When your lovebird is adjusted to your home and doesn't fly away or squawk at you when you approach his cage, it's time to begin training him. Take your bird and his cage, along with a small dowel you will use as a perch, into a small room, such as the bathroom, and place the cage on the floor. Also, take along some of his favorite treats to give him as a reward for good behavior. If you do choose the bathroom, close the toilet lid and the shower stall doors and sit down on the floor next to the cage.

Open the cage door and put the dowel inside. Position it so that it is in front of your lovebird. As you do so, say, "Step up," which he will probably do automatically. Remove him from his cage on the dowel.

If your bird doesn't willingly step onto the perch, remove it from the cage and leave the cage door

open. Allow your bird to come out on his own and investigate the room, or offer him some of his favorite treats to tempt him out of his cage. Place the dowel in front of your lovebird, and try nudging him in the abdomen again, repeating the "step up" command as you do so. Praise him if he steps onto the perch, then pick up the perch slowly and hold it at mid-chest level. Let the bird sit on the dowel for a few minutes, then take him over to the top of his cage and gently rotate the perch so that he steps onto the cage top. Say, "Step down," as he does so. Repeat this exercise one more time during the first training session. Give him a treat to reward his good behavior.

If your bird doesn't step onto the

dowel immediately, don't chase him around the room with it. Talk to him in a calm, cheerful voice to allow him to calm down. Give him a treat when he's calm.

End the first training session after about 15 minutes, whether or not your bird steps onto the perch. Return him to his cage, give him a treat, and praise him for being a good bird. Repeat the training session each day until he steps up onto the perch with confidence.

Teaching your bird to step up and step down helps you maintain control over him. If he gets himself into trouble in your home, you can place your hand in front of him and tell him to "step up" before you return him to his cage for a little corrective "time-out."

After your lovebird has mastered the "step up" and "step down" commands, he's ready to move on to the really fun part of bird training: learning tricks.

For My Next Trick...

Trick training builds on the trust you've established with your lovebird. Trick training works best if you can use a behavior your bird already does naturally and build it into a trick. For instance, if your lovebird likes picking things up in his beak, he may be a good candidate to learn to drop coins into a bank. If he willingly lies in your hand on his back, he may quickly learn how to play dead or roll over.

Work with your lovebird to develop unique tricks the two of you can perform. You'll enjoy teaching your bird to do something that no other bird does, and your bird will enjoy learning something new to do too.

Solving Problem Behaviors

Lovebirds and other pet birds can be prone to four major behavior problems—biting, screaming, chewing, and feather picking. We'll look briefly at the possible causes and some solutions for each.

Keep in mind that this brief look at behavior problems only scratches the surface, so be sure to discuss any behavior problems your bird has with your veterinarian. She may have a behaviorist on staff or be able to refer you to someone in your area who is trained to deal with avian behavior problems.

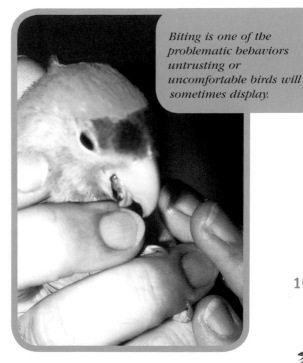

Biting is one of the problematic behaviors untrusting or uncomfortable birds will sometimes display.

Biting

Causes include fear, stress, or a desire to breed. It is also common among juvenile birds exploring their world or birds who don't understand their place in your family's flock. Possible solutions include regaining your bird's trust, setting him up with a mate, or giving him the opportunity to explore his world more fully under supervision. You can also train him not to bite using positive reinforcement.

Screaming

Causes include stress, being rewarded for screaming in the past, a desire to breed, boredom, or isolation. Possible solutions include reducing your bird's stress level, giving him positive

If your bird spends a lot of time screaming, he could be stressed out, bored, lonely, or even looking to mate.

reinforcement when he's good instead of rewarding him for screaming in the future, getting him a mate, getting him a wider variety of toys, or relocating his cage to a part of the house that lets him feel more like he's part of the family.

Chewing
The most common problem with chewing is that your lovebird chews on things he isn't supposed to, like the leg of your coffee table or the frame around your grandmother's photo on a family room end table. The problem here isn't chewing but rather supervision. The best solution for chewing is to provide your lovebird with plenty of safe and appropriate chew toys and to prevent him from chewing on things you don't want him

to chew. Keep in mind that chewing is a normal behavior that lovebirds need to do each day to keep their beaks in condition.

Feather Picking

Causes include illnesses, stress, up care, the reduction of stress in the bird's environment, providing the bird with a variety of interesting toys, or setting the bird up with a mate. This is a difficult behavior problem to solve; consider hiring an avian behavior consultant.

Being Good

Resources

CLUBS & SOCIETIES

African Lovebird Society
PO Box 7312
San Marcos, CA 92079-0142
www.africanlovebirdsociety.com

American Federation of Aviculture, Inc.
P.O. Box 7312
N. Kansas City, MO 64116
Phone:(816) 421-2473
Fax: (816) 421-3214
afaoffice@aol.com
www.AFAbirds.org

Avicultural Society of America
Secretary: Helen Hanson
info@asabirds.org
www.asabirds.org

VETERINARY RESOURCES

American Board of Veterinary Practitioners (ABVP)
618 Church Street, Suite 220
Nashville, TN 37219
Phone: (800) 697-3583, (615) 250-7794
Fax: (615) 254-7047
abvp@xmi-amc.com
www.abvp.com

American Veterinary Medical Association (AVMA)
1931 North Meacham Road-Suite 100
Schaumburg, IL 60173
E-mail: avmainfo@avma.org
www.avma.org

Animal Behavior Society
Indiana University
2611 East 10th Street #170
Bloomington IN 47408-2603
Telephone: (812) 856-5541
E-mail: aboffice@indiana.edu
www.animalbehavior.org

Association of Avian Veterinarians (AAV)
P.O. Box 811720
Boca Raton, FL 33481-1720
Phone: (561) 393-8901
Fax: (561) 393-8902
AAVCTRLOFC@aol.com
www.aav.org

British Veterinary Association (BVA)
7 Mansfield Street
London
W1G 9NQ
Telephone: 020 7636 6541
Fax: 020 7436 2970
E-mail: bvahq@bva.co.uk
www.bva.co.uk

EMERGENCY RESOURCES

ASPCA Animal Poison Control Center
Phone: (888) 426-4435
napcc@aspca.org (for general information only)
www.apcc.aspca.org

Bird Hotline
P.O. Box 1411
Sedona, AZ 86339-1411
birdhotline@birdhotline.com
www.birdhotline.com

Rescue & Adoption Organizations

American Humane Association (AHA)
63 Inverness Drive East
Englewood, CO 80112
Telephone: (303) 792-9900
Fax: 792-5333
www.americanhumane.org

American Society for the Prevention of Cruelty to Animals (ASPCA)
424 E. 92nd Street
New York, NY 10128-6804
Phone: (212) 876-7700
www.aspca.org

Best Friends Animal Sanctuary
5001 Angel Canyon Road
Kanab, UT 84741-5001
Phone: (435) 644-2001
info@bestfriends.org
www.bestfriends.com

Bird Placement Program
P.O. Box 347392
Parma, OH, 44134-7392
Phone: (330) 772-1627 or (216) 749-3643
www.avi-sci.com/bpp/

For the Love of Parrots Refuge Society
3450 Interporvincial Highway
Abbotsford, British Columbia
Phone: (604) 854-8180 or (604) 854-8381

Foster Parrots Ltd.
P.O. Box 650
Rockland, MA, 02370
Phone: (781) 878-3733
www.fosterparrots.com

Gabriel Foundation
P.O. Box 11477
Aspen, CO 81612
Phone: (877) 923-1009
www.thegabrielfoundation.org

Oasis Sanctuary
P.O. Box 3104
Scottsdale, AZ 85271
www.the-oasis.org

Royal Society for the Prevention of Cruelty to Animals (RSPCA)
Telephone: 0870 3335 999
Fax: 0870 7530 284
www.rspca.org.uk

The Blue Cross
Shilton Road
Burford
Oxon OX18 4PF
England
Phone: 44 01993 825500
info@bluecross.org.uk
www.bluecross.org.uk

Tropics Exotic Bird Refuge
P.O. Box 686
Kannapolis, NC 28082-0686
Phone: (704) 932-8041 or (704) 634-9066
tropics@juno.com

WEB SITES

Avian Network
www.aviannetwork.com

Avian Web
www.avianweb.com

Birdy Works
www.birdyworks.com

The Lovebird Information Center
www.lovebirdcenter.com

The Lovebird Society (UK)
www.lovebirdsociety.co.uk

PUBLICATIONS

Magazines
Bird Talk
3 Burroughs
Irvine, CA 92618
Phone: (949) 855-8822
Fax: (949) 855-3045
www.animalnetwork.com/birdtalk/
default.asp

Bird Times
7-L Dundas Circle
Greensboro, NC 27407
Phone: (336)292-4047

Good Bird
PO Box 684394
Austin, TX 78768
Phone: (512) 423-7734
or (512) 236-0531
info@goodbirdinc.com
www.GoodBirdInc.com

Pet Bird Report
2236 Mariner Square Drive, No. 35
Alameda, CA 94501
Phone: (510) 523-5303
www.petbirdreport.com

Winged Wisdom
Birds n Ways
39760 Calle Bellagio
Temecula, CA 92592
Phone: (909) 303-9376

Books
Boruchowitz, David E., *The Guide to Owning a Lovebird*, TFH Publications.

Moustaki, Nikki, *A New Owner's Guide to Lovebirds*, TFH Publications.

Moustaki, Nikki, *Your Outta Control Bird*, TFH Publications.

O'Connor, Rebecca K., *A Parrot for Life*, TFH Publications.

Index

Note: Boldfaced numbers indicate illustrations.

Dedication

To Loren Jackson and Jim Hayes. Thanks for believing in me and always encouraging me to do better!

About the Author

Julie Mancini has authored numerous books and magazine and online articles, with animals as her primary focus. Julie has had many companion animals, including several parrots. A freelance writer for the past 10 years, Julie and her husband currently live on a small farm in south-central Iowa.

Photo Credits

REACH OUT. ACT. RESPOND.
Go to AnimalPlanet.com/ROAR and find out how
you can be a voice for animals everywhere!